BRIDGING
English Language Learners to GED® Test Prep

TEACHER'S GUIDE

Reasoning Through Language Arts

Lia Conklin Olson

ProLiteracy
New Readers Press®

Bridging English Language Learners for GED® Test Prep: Reasoning Through Language Arts
ISBN 978-1-56420-077-8

Published by New Readers Press, a division of ProLiteracy.

Printed in the United States of America
10   9   8   7

Proceeds from the sale of New Readers Press materials support professional
development, training, and technical assistance programs of ProLiteracy
that benefit local literacy programs in the U.S. and around the globe.

Editor: Laura McLoughlin
Editorial Director: Terrie Lipke
Designer: Cathi Miller
Technology Specialist: Maryellen Casey

CONTENTS

CONTENTS

Check and Revise

Timed Extended-Response Practice

Short Answer Responses

APPENDICES

Note: This book refers to lessons and page numbers in the 2016 editions of *Writing for the GED® Test*. If using an earlier edition of *Writing for the GED® Test 3: Extended Response and Short Answers*, page numbers may not match.

About *Bridging English Language Learners to GED® Test Prep*

Why *Bridging*?

If our GED classrooms were filled with students reading at the 11th- and 12th-grade level, there would be no need for this book. Guiding students as they read through the New Readers Press GED preparation materials would be enough. The reality is, of course, that by and large students come to us for GED preparation with reading levels far below that. When we add to that the increasing number of English language learners (ELLs) with language development needs, preparing our learners for the GED test becomes quite a challenge. The good news is we have a job to do—and an important one! The better news is that this teacher's guide can help us bridge our ELLs from where they are to where they need to be. A wise man (Lev Vygotsky) once hypothesized that there is a zone of proximal development in which a knowledgeable other (that's you) could push students from where they are to greater levels of knowledge. It is with this in mind that *Bridging* was born.

ELLs come to us with an abundance of skills, and it is up to us to attach trusses of learning to those skills to provide access to GED preparation even when their reading levels are "too" low or their language skills are "too" underdeveloped. As the *knowledgeable others*, we can provide learning opportunities that bridge these gaps to open opportunities for students to learn GED content. This teacher's guide is intended for instructors of students reading at a sixth-grade level or above whose productive (oral and written) language development is lagging behind. That said, we all know that students with lower reading levels come through our doors eager to do what they need to do to get their GEDs. Although it is unlikely that a student reading at a sixth-grade reading level will pass the GED test, it is possible that providing these trusses of learning will not only allow them access to GED prep materials but may also increase their reading level and language development sufficiently that by the time they take the test, they may have the skills they need to be successful. So open up this teacher's guide and embrace your ELLs and their language needs. With a little prep, you can begin to bridge their journey to the GED.

What's in *Bridging*?

This guide provides:

- Lessons that correspond to and support each reading and writing lesson of the New Readers Press *Writing for the GED Test* series
- Skills-based questions to focus each lesson and guiding questions to contextualize each lesson
- Learning goals that are clearly defined and aligned to GED targets
- Instructional strategies that support students' knowledge-building, reading, vocabulary development, and written responses
- References to pre-GED resources that bridge learners' prior knowledge to GED content
- Example instructional activities that model instructional strategies
- Vocabulary development strategies that include word study and usage

Materials Needed to Use this Book

Bridging for Reasoning through Language Arts follows the New Readers Press *Writing for the GED Test* books 1 through 3. This book's lessons follow the lessons in each book and link to other New Readers Press materials to build on the content and skills required on the GED test. These books are available to purchase at newreaderspress.com.

This teacher's guide uses these New Readers Press materials (referred to throughout this text as *Writing* book 1, *Writing* book 2, and *Writing* book 3):

- *Writing for the GED® Test 1: Grammar, Usage, and Mechanics*
- *Writing for the GED® Test 2: Reading Comprehension*
- *Writing for the GED® Test 3: Extended Response and Short Answers*

Corresponding materials:

- *Core Skills in Reading and Writing*
- *Core Skills in Science*
- *Scoreboost for the GED® Test: Responding to Text on the Language Arts and Science Tests*
- *Scoreboost for the GED® Test: Sentence Structure, Usage, and Mechanics*
- *Scoreboost for the GED® Test: Critical Thinking for Reading, Science, and Social Studies*
- *Pre-HSE Workbook: Reading* (Comprehension and Critical Thinking)
- *Pre-HSE Workbook: Writing 1* (Grammar, Spelling, and Writing Basics)
- *Pre-HSE Workbook: Writing 2* (Developing and Organizing Written Responses)

How Does *Bridging* Work?

This graphic illustrates the relationship between all of the components of *Bridging*.

Reading Informational Texts

INFERENCES AND CONCLUSIONS

Skills-Based Questions

1. How have historical documents shaped the American government? *(Part 1)*

2. How have U.S. Supreme Court rulings shaped American institutions and public policy? *(Part 2)*

Bridging Language Usage Strategies

- Language usage activities that target integration and student accountability

Language Usage Goals

Bridging Knowledge Strategies

- References to pre-GED materials
- Guiding questions

Knowledge Goals

Learning Goals

Reading Goals

Bridging Reading Strategies

- Example instructional activities

Vocabulary Goals

Written Response Goals

Bridging Vocabulary Strategies

- Vocabulary practices that target word study and usage

Bridging Written Response Strategies

- Example instructional activities

> ### Skills-Based Questions

Each lesson begins with Skills-Based Questions to focus the lesson on specific skills within the language arts content area. Providing an overview of the skill development students can expect in the form of a question allows students to assess themselves once the lesson is completed.

> ### Learning Goals

Learning Goals, the knowledge and skills students will be able to demonstrate upon completion of the lesson, are listed in student-friendly language for five categories of learning: Knowledge, Reading, Vocabulary, Written Response, and Language Usage. All learning goals are directly tied to the GED Assessment Targets for Reasoning Through Language Arts in the areas of Reading, Writing, and Language. (You can find these targets online in the Assessment Guide for Educators at gedtestingservice.com.)

Here is an example of this from the Inferences and Conclusions lesson in the Reading Informational Texts unit of *Writing for the GED® Test* book 2.

	Learning Goals	GED Assessment Targets	GED
Knowledge Goals:	1. Understand how to make inferences and draw conclusions.		R.2.3
	2. Compare and contrast inferences and conclusions.		R.2.8
Reading Goals:	1. Make inferences about supporting details.		R.2.3
	2. Draw conclusions or make generalizations based on the main ideas in a text.		R.2.8
Vocabulary Goals:	1. Define key subject and academic vocabulary.		R.4.1
	2. Determine the meaning of unknown vocabulary using context clues, word forms, and parts of speech.		
	3. Produce writing and speech using new vocabulary.		
Written Response Goals:	1. Determine what is stated in the text and make logical inferences or conclusions supported by text evidence.		W.1
	2. Respond to text by summarizing events clearly, organizing information logically, supporting conclusions with examples, and focusing on the writing task.		W.2 W.3
	3. Write using standard English conventions. *(See Language Usage Goals)*		
Language Usage Goals:	1. Identify the subject and predicate and correct subject/predicate order.		L.1.5
	2. Edit writing to include complete sentences with the correct subject/predicate order.		L.1.6

Sample Instructional Support Strategies

ELLs often struggle in five key areas of GED preparation: Knowledge, Reading, Vocabulary, Written Response, and Language Usage. *Bridging* focuses on instructional strategies in each of these areas that help ELLs access GED preparation content. The bolded instructional strategies in each box indicate which strategies are used in that lesson. The examples are numbered to correspond with the strategies they represent.

➢ Bridging Knowledge

ELLs often lack the background knowledge, both cultural and content-related, that many native-born GED students have. Providing them with resources to bridge this gap is essential for their success with the GED prep materials. Here are the instructional strategies to focus on when bridging the knowledge gap.

> **Strategy 1:** **Develop background knowledge to connect to new knowledge.**
>
> **Strategy 2:** **Use guiding questions to make connections beyond the lesson to broader life themes and topics.**
>
> Strategy 3: Use reading strategies to develop, monitor, and synthesize new knowledge. *(See Bridging Reading)*
>
> **Strategy 4:** **Demonstrate synthesis of new knowledge through a variety of student response tasks.** *(See Bridging Student Response)*

In this book, some strategies are bolded and some are not. The bold strategies are the ones used in that lesson. Examples that follow are numbered to match the strategies they represent.

1. *Bridging* provides references to corresponding New Readers Press pre-GED and GED materials to bridge students' background knowledge to the material covered in the *Writing* series. Here is an example:

Inferences and Conclusions	Reading Inferences Drawing Conclusions	Writing Summary Conclusions	Language Usage Subject/Predicates
Writing for the GED Test Book 1: Grammar, Usage, and Mechanics			Basic Sentence Parts (p. 20); Nouns and Personal Pronouns (p. 38); Verb Tenses and Forms (p. 42)
Core Skills in Reading & Writing	Unit 3, Lesson 4: Drawing Conclusions (p. 65); Lesson 6: Summarizing (p. 71)	Unit 5, Lesson 1: Topic Sentences (p. 115); Lesson 2: Supporting Details (p. 118); Lesson 3: Transitions (p. 121)	Unit 4: Lesson 1: Parts of Speech (p. 80); Lesson 2: Sentence Structure (p. 84)
Scoreboost: Writing Across the Tests Sentence Structure, Usage, and Mechanics (SS); Responding to Text (RT)		RT: Summarize Main Idea or Theme (p. 31) [Science related]	
Scoreboost: Thinking Skills Critical Thinking	Make Inferences (p. 8); Draw Conclusions (p. 20)	Summarize Ideas (p. 6); Draw Conclusions (p. 20)	
Pre-HSE Workbook Reading (R); Writing 1 (W1); Writing 2 (W2)	R: Inferences and Conclusions (p. 14)		W1: Parts of a Sentence (p. 12); Basic Verb Tenses & Forms (p. 24)

2. **Guiding Questions:** Each lesson contains Guiding Questions that situate the lesson content within a line of inquiry. A line of inquiry is simply a learning pathway that begins with a relevant question and guides students along a path to discover its answer. Unlike the Skills-Based Questions at the beginning of the lesson that focus on specific language arts skills, guiding questions draw students deeper into the lesson and allow them to make connections beyond the content of the lesson. Here are two examples from the Inferences and Conclusions lesson:

   1. What can you conclude from the text about settling the West in the 1800s?

   2. How do the details of the text support your conclusion?

> **Bridging Reading**

Compared to many native-born GED students, ELLs have often had less exposure to English text and less internalization of the English language structures found in text. Teaching strategies that help students develop, monitor, and synthesize their understanding of text is key to ELLs accessing GED prep materials and increasing their reading levels. Here are four instructional strategies focused on in *Bridging*:

Strategy 1: *Determine the type of text, establish reading purpose, and make predictions using text features and signal words.*

Strategy 2: *Develop text analysis using think-alouds, annotation, sentence frames, and graphic organizers.*

Strategy 3: *Overcome text analysis barriers using prior knowledge, analyzing language usage, and using resources.*

Strategy 4: *Synthesize text analysis using paraphrasing, text frames, graphic organizers, and peer discussions.*

Of primary importance is teaching students the following five reading strategies.

• **Pre-reading strategies:** Strategies that orient students to the features of the text by scanning the text for the title, headings, bullets, vocabulary terms in bold or italics, signal words (words that signal the purpose of the text, such as cause and effect, compare and contrast, etc.), any visuals included with the text, and any questions/directions/prompts that accompany the text. Students can use this preview to determine the type of text, its purpose, the purpose of the reading task, and to make predictions about what they will be reading. Given only a few obvious text features or clues, students may scan the first paragraph for the topic sentence to refine their predictions. You may want students to do this activity before you share the learning goals in order that they generate their own learning goals for the lesson.

- **Annotation:** A step-by-step process by which students make notes to extract meaning with each subsequent reading of the text. *Bridging* uses one variation of annotation grounded in Close Reading principles and developed over time through the author's trial and error in her own classroom. These steps may be somewhat different depending on the purpose of the text but basically students move from general understanding (gist) to detailed understanding through subsequent readings of the text:

  1. **First Reading:** Students read for gist and note the overall main idea of the passage including who/what it's about, where and when (especially for narratives and fictional texts) it takes place, and in general what happened, resulted, or was described (what = conflict and resolution for short stories) and why or how (if applicable).

     > *Annotations for gist for non-fiction (in margins or notebook):*
     >
     > *Who/what:* Pluto
     >
     > *Where/when:* 2006 in the U.S.
     >
     > *What:* demoted to a dwarf planet
     >
     > *Why:* new criteria; has debris in its orbit

     > *Annotations for gist for short stories (in margins or notebook):*
     >
     > *Who:* Cherokee boys and mothers
     >
     > *Where/when:* in their town when the earth was young
     >
     > *What (conflict):* The boys are playing too much and not helping their families so the mothers are angry
     >
     > *What (resolution):* The boys become the constellation the Pleiades; one becomes the pine tree

  2. **Second Reading:** Students identify the topic sentence of each paragraph/section, the definitions of important terms, and confusing words, phrases, and/or sentences of the text. Students note who/what (agent), where/when (if applicable), what (happened/resulted/ was described), and why/how (if applicable) for each paragraph/section of the text.

     > *Annotation Scheme:*
     >
     > <u>Underline</u> or highlight: topic sentences
     >
     > <u>Double underline</u> or highlight (new color): definitions
     >
     > Circle and write a (?): confusing words, phrases, and/or sentences.

  3. **Third Reading:** Students return to confusing areas of the text to interpret unknown words using vocabulary strategies and to dissect confusing, complex sentences for subject/agent (underline), verb/action (double underline), phrases (circle), and dependent clauses that provide detailed information. For many sentences, it is helpful for comprehension to keep the complete subject together and the complete predicate together, rather than isolating the simple subject and verb.

     > *Sentence Dissection:*
     >
     > Some <u>specialized cells</u> <u>work</u> (with other cells) like them, [the way that a number of <u>carpenters</u> may <u>work</u> (together on a house)].

- **Text frames:** Fill-in-the-blank frames at the sentence or paragraph level provide the language and language structure that match the writing purpose. Bridging draws from the work of Jeff Zwiers in this respect. Appendix B (p. 136) provides a list of signal words that support this process.

- **Graphic organizers:** Visual organization of text information aids in developing, monitoring, and synthesizing the understanding of text. Graphic organizers provide additional and varied opportunities for students to develop deeper understanding of text both through recognizing different learning styles and reinforcing information in different ways.

- **Think-alouds:** Students (and teachers) share aloud the thinking processes they use to extract meaning from the text. Think-alouds give students the opportunity to express the mental actions they are using to make, monitor, and synthesize meaning. Through this sharing, not only are teachers able to see where students are succeeding and faltering, but students become aware of their own processing and gain exposure to the successful processing of others.

➤ Bridging Vocabulary

Vocabulary building for ELLs is critical for success in GED preparation. *Bridging* focuses on two categories of vocabulary: content vocabulary and academic vocabulary. Content vocabulary refers to subject-related words that are often exclusive to a subject area or have a particular meaning within a subject area. Academic vocabulary, on the other hand, refers to words that are used in all sorts of academic texts and discussions, regardless of the specific subject matter. Whichever the vocabulary type, students must not only be able to understand the word when they read it but also be able to use it in oral and written contexts. Repeat exposure to and practice of vocabulary words in a variety of ways and in a variety of contexts is key to developing productive use of vocabulary. Here are some instructional strategies for providing the kinds of exposure and practice ELLs need to add new words to their productive vocabulary.

Strategy 1: *Identify the component parts and parts of speech of new words to interpret their meanings.*

Strategy 2: *Use context clues to interpret new words, including figurative and connotative language.*

Strategy 3: *Utilize vocabulary-building resources.*

Strategy 4: *Build a deeper knowledge of words through writing and speaking tasks.*

Vocabulary Development Lists in Appendix C (p. 138) contain lists of target content and academic words for each reading and writing lesson of *Writing* books 2 and 3. Each lesson contains an alphabetized list of content words that help students develop knowledge within the language arts area. In addition, eight academic words of more general use are included (for all lessons that feature a reading passage) with their usage and syllabic and word-part breakdown. Academic words are generated from the featured readings in that lesson and focus on words that are important within the topic of that lesson and have wider academic use. For example, if the lesson focuses on character development, then targeted words may be adjectives that both describe characters and are common in a variety of academic contexts.

Appendix D (p. 144) provides a template for students to capture the types of practices suggested in the Bridging Vocabulary strategies. Students will fill in the template with information for the target words of each lesson as you lead them through the following strategies:

1. First, present the shortest form of the word (the base word, often the verb form), followed by other commonly used word forms (if available). Examine prefixes and suffixes and their impact on word meaning and usage.

2. Read the word as it is used in the context of the text and discuss possible meanings given context clues and word form.

3. Have students find (electronically or in print) the definition or translation of the base form and, if different, the form used in context and note these definitions in the space provided for future reference and study.

4. Gradually build a deeper knowledge of the word by having students use the word in a sentence frame, guided discussion, and an original sentence.

Template Example:

Word or **phrase** (usage) [syl • lab • ic breakdown]	**Word Family** (usage) [*prefix* • base word • *suffix*]	**Synonym**
protect (verb) [pro • tect]	protec*tion* (noun) protec*tive* (adjective)	guard
Definition/Translation: *(Student generated)*		
In Context:	"…many people were expressing concerns that the document did not provide sufficient **protection** for the civil liberties of citizens."	
Sentence Frame:	I must protect my _____ from _____.	
Guided Discussion:	What are some ways you protect yourself from danger?	
Original Sentence:	*(Student generated)*	

In addition to the content and academic words targeted in the lessons, *Bridging* contains a list of test-taking words (p. 137) that show up in the GED test and prep materials. It is crucial that students have working knowledge of these words. Providing a reference list for students to study and refer to will greatly enhance their ability to participate in GED prep practices and activities.

➢ Bridging Written Response

Perhaps more than any other area, student response is where ELLs fall behind their native-born counterparts. Research shows that receptive learning (reading and listening) develops more quickly and more easily than productive learning (speaking and writing). However, student response is critical for passing the GED and, of course, for success in life in general. The following instructional strategies are highlighted in *Bridging*:

> **Strategy 1:** *Prepare for a response task by identifying its purpose, audience, signal words, structure, and style.*
>
> **Strategy 2:** *Organize text analysis for written response using a graphic organizer and/or paragraph/essay frame.*
>
> **Strategy 3:** *Overcome barriers to producing clear/coherent writing by using models, language analysis, and resources.*
>
> **Strategy 4:** *Revise writing by utilizing peer- and self-editing checklists, rubrics, and writing resources.*
>
> **Strategy 5*:** *Extend text analysis to build upon initial information or claims by using evidence from additional sources.*

* For lessons in *Writing* book 2 only

Bridging Written Response uses some of the same strategies used in Bridging Reading, such as utilizing annotations from reading activities, developing graphic organizers, and using text frames (at the paragraph level). However, using models of student written response, collaborative work (including evaluation and editing), and extended research (for reading comprehension) are included to deepen understanding of the content and support a higher-quality response.

- Collaborative work both mirrors real life and work situations and provides students the practice they need in productive language. Collaborative work allows students to negotiate, clarify, and build deeper meaning than working on their own. This not only requires the use of productive language but higher order thinking skills as well. Appendix B (p. 136) provides a list of discourse prompts used for varying purposes within collaborative work.

- Peer and self evaluation help students become aware of the quality of their written responses, utilize strategies to improve the quality, and hold students accountable for their own writing progress. *Bridging* includes two tools to help students in this process:

  1. The Extended-Response Evaluation Rubric (p. 132) can be used to evaluate the components of a student's (or a peer's) written response by reviewing each of the 10 areas while following the suggested editing actions and scoring the level of mastery.

  2. The Editing Rubric (p. 131) provides a list of all the sentence structure, grammar and usage, and mechanics areas that are evaluated on the GED test. Students can use this tool to guide them in editing their own writing or that of a peer by following the steps outlined in the rubric to evaluate language usage. (See Bridging Language Usage Strategy 4 for further details.)

- GED prep materials provide only foundational information for each of the key reading, writing, and language usage areas, therefore, there are times that students need additional research or investigation to better develop understanding of the topic. Furthermore, additional research allows students to apply and connect their knowledge to other situations making the learning more relevant and meaningful.

➤ Bridging Language Usage

> **Strategy 1:** *Determine and target areas of language usage that require further development.*
>
> **Strategy 2:** *Analyze specific areas of language usage as modeled in authentic and relevant communication tasks.*
>
> **Strategy 3:** *Develop specific areas of language usage through participation in authentic communication tasks.*
>
> **Strategy 4:** *Revise language usage by utilizing peer- and self-editing checklists, rubrics, and language resources.*

1–2. Developing language usage in its various facets (sentence structure, grammar, mechanics, etc.) is most effective when practiced within authentic communicative activities or tasks. The best way to do this is to provide "just-in-time" mini-lessons on language usage topics (the parts) within the main learning activities of reading, writing, and conversation (the whole). "Just-in-time" mini-lessons focus on areas of language usage that students struggle with in the context of the main activity of the lesson. The Language Usage Checklist (p. 129) is a tool that can help students set and monitor their language usage goals.

If you are thinking, "But my students need *everything* just-in-time!" you are not alone. In fact, if this is true for your students, you are at an advantage. Given groups of students with similar language needs, you can plan ahead and determine which language usage areas to integrate into which tasks. If this is not the case, responding to students' needs and language goals day-to-day may be your most effective option.

3. *Bridging* provides contextualization of language usage practice in three ways:

    1. By providing suggestions on responding to students' needs and goals as they are revealed during lessons and tasks

    2. By integrating the different lessons from *Writing* book 1 into the *Bridging* lesson plans for *Writing* book 2

    3. By integrating the language usage lessons from *Writing* book 3's Check and Revise unit into the Read and Analyze and Plan and Write units of the same book.

    Whichever direction you take, you are providing an effective way for your students to develop their language usage through integration.

    In addition, *Bridging* references the *Writing* book 1 practices in the Bridging Knowledge section of the *Writing* book 3 lessons as a strategy for building students' background knowledge of language usage.

4. Self and peer editing are tried-and-true ways to help students become aware of their language errors, utilize strategies to revise them, and be accountable for the quality of their own writing. *Bridging* includes two tools to help students in this process.

    1. The Language Usage Checklist (p. 129) provides a list of all the sentence structure, grammar and usage, and mechanics areas that are evaluated on the GED test. Students can set a language goal, follow the listed actions to practice that language usage area, and note when their language goal is met.

    2. The Editing Rubric (p. 131) mentioned in Bridging Written Response can be used to evaluate their own language usage, or that of a peer, by reviewing each of the 10 areas, while following the editing actions and scoring the level of mastery.

All Lessons

ALL LESSONS

Skills-Based Questions:

1. How do you write using standard English language conventions such as sentence structure, grammar, and mechanics?

2. How do you revise your writing to correct errors in sentence structure, grammar, and mechanics?

	Learning Goals:	**GED**
Knowledge Goals:	1. Identify proper use of sentence structure, grammar, and mechanics.	
Reading Goals:	1. Determine how parts of the text (words, phrases, clauses, and paragraphs) fit into the structure and message of the complete text.	R.5.1
	2. Describe how parts of the text (words, phrases, clauses, and paragraphs) relate to other parts of the text.	R.5.2
	3. Identify signal words that show relationships in the text and determine how they affect the meaning and/or purpose of the text.	R.5.3
	4. Determine how a section of the text affects meaning or supports the author's purpose.	R.5.4
Vocabulary Goals:	1. Determine meaning of unknown vocabulary using word forms, and parts of speech.	R.4.1
	2. Identify and correct errors involving commonly confused words.	L.1.1
Written Response Goals:	1. Use standard English grammar, punctuation, and mechanics. *(See Language Usage Goals)*	W.3
Language Usage Goals:	1. Identify and correct errors involving commonly confused words.	L.1.1
	2. Identify and correct errors in subject-verb agreement.	L.1.2
	3. Identify and correct errors in pronoun usage.	L.1.3
	4. Identify and replace informal usage with standard English.	L.1.4
	5. Identify and correct word order.	L.1.5
	6. Edit to include correct complex sentences.	L.1.6
	7. Identify and correct errors in complex subject-verb agreement and pronoun usage.	L.1.7
	8. Identify and improve unnecessary repetition and unclear sentence structure.	L.1.8
	9. Edit to include appropriate "signal words" for transitions and relationships between ideas and sentences.	L.1.9
	10. Identify and correct errors in capitalization.	L.2.1
	11. Identify and correct improper sentence structure with correct punctuation.	L.2.2
	12. Edit to include correct use of apostrophes.	L.2.3
	13. Identify and correct errors in punctuation.	L.2.4

➤ Bridging Knowledge

See the Bridging Language Usage Cross-Reference Guide (p. 133) for a complete cross-referenced list of New Readers Press grammar resources that support GED preparation.

➤ Bridging Reading

See the *Bridging* lessons that support *Writing for the GED Test 2: Reading Comprehension* (beginning on page 16) for ways to integrate language usage areas into reading activities.

➤ Bridging Vocabulary

Familiarize students with language usage vocabulary as they practice each area. Specific vocabulary leads to identification of language usage areas that lead to awareness of problem areas, which in turn results in corrections and a progressive mastery of language usage.

➤ Bridging Written Response

See the *Bridging* lessons that support *Writing for the GED Test 2: Reading Comprehension* and *Writing for the GED Test 3: Extended Response and Short Answers* for ways to integrate language usage areas into writing activities.

➤ Bridging Language Usage

> **Strategy 1:** *Determine and target areas of language usage that require further development.*
>
> **Strategy 2:** *Analyze specific areas of language usage as modeled in authentic and relevant communication tasks.*
>
> **Strategy 3:** *Develop specific areas of language usage through participation in authentic communication tasks.*
>
> **Strategy 4:** *Revise language usage by utilizing peer- and self-editing checklists, rubrics, and language resources.*

1-2. As mentioned in the introduction, the development of each aspect of language usage is most effective when practiced through authentic communicative activities or tasks. Think of the various facets of language usage (sentence structure, grammar, mechanics, etc.) as the individual parts that make up the larger ability to comprehend reading, writing, and conversation. The best way to develop language usage is to provide "just-in-time" mini-lessons within the context of the main activity of the lesson. The Language Usage Checklist (p. 129) is a tool that can help students set and monitor their language usage goals.

3. *Bridging* provides contextualization of language usage practice in *Writing* book 1 in two ways:

   1. By providing suggestions on responding to students' needs and goals as they are revealed during lessons and assessments

   2. By integrating the different lessons from *Writing* book 1 into the *Bridging* lesson plans for *Writing* book 2

   Whichever direction you take, you are providing an effective way for your students to develop their language usage through integration.

The following grid illustrates how *Bridging* integrates language usage with the reading lessons in *Writing* book 2. This sequence was developed by first considering the content and concepts being developed in the reading lessons and matching them to particular sentence structure practices from *Writing* book 1. Then these practices were linked to grammar and mechanics practices from the same text. You may very well find a different sequence that works better for your students, but here's a start.

Writing for the GED Test book 2 Reading Lessons	Writing for the GED Test book 1 Sentence Structure Practices	Grammar & Mechanics Practices
1. Inferences and Conclusions (p. 6)	Basic Sentence Parts (p. 20)	Nouns and Personal Pronouns (p. 38) Verb Tenses and Forms (p. 42)
2. Main Ideas and Supporting Details (p. 12)	Simple and Compound Sentences (p. 22)	Irregular Verbs (p. 44) Subject-Verb Agreement I (p. 48)
3. Sequence of Events (p. 18)	Complex Sentences (p. 24)	The Perfect Tenses (p. 46) Subject-Verb Agreement II (p. 50) Commas (p. 66)
4. Comparisons and Contrasts (p. 24)	Simple and Compound Sentences (p. 22) Complex Sentences (p. 24)	Other Kinds of Pronouns (p. 40) Subject-Verb Agreement II (p. 50)
5. Cause-and-Effect Relationships (p. 30)	Sentence Fragments (p. 26)	Subject-Verb Agreement III (p. 52) Semicolons (p. 68) Commas (p. 66)
6. Language: Meaning and Tone (p. 36)	Run-ons and Comma Splices (p. 28)	Commas (p. 66) Semicolons (p. 68)
7. Plot (p. 46)	Sentence Fragments (p. 26) Run-ons and Comma Splices (p. 28)	Subject-Verb Agreement I–III (pp. 48–52) Other Kinds of Pronouns (p. 40)
8. Character (p. 52)	Parallelism and Coordination (p. 30)	Pronoun-Antecedent Agreement (p. 54) Clear Antecedents (p. 56)
9. Theme (p. 58)	Misplaced Modifiers (p. 32) Dangling Modifiers (p. 34)	Plurals and Possessives (p. 70)
10. Figurative Language (p. 64)	Informal and Nonstandard Usage (p. 58) Wordy and Awkward Writing (p. 60)	Capitalization (p. 64) Words That Sound Alike (p. 72)

Note: An integration sequence for the writing lessons in *Writing* book 3 is not provided since that text contains language usage practice within its Check and Revise unit. However, *Bridging* does reference *Writing* book 1 in the Bridging Knowledge section of each writing lesson as a strategy for building students' background knowledge of language usage.

4. Self and peer editing are tried-and-true ways to help students become aware of their language errors, utilize strategies to revise them, and be accountable for the quality of their own writing. *Bridging* includes two tools to help students in this process. One is the Language Usage Checklist (p. 129) mentioned previously. This provides a list of all the sentence structure, grammar and usage, and mechanics areas that are evaluated on the GED test. Students can set a language goal, follow the listed actions to practice that language usage area, and note when their language goal is met. The second tool is the Editing Rubric (p. 131). Students can use this to evaluate their own language usage or that of a peer by reviewing each of the 10 areas, following the editing actions, and scoring the level of mastery.

Reading Informational Texts

INFERENCES AND CONCLUSIONS

Skills-Based Questions

1. What can we infer from a text segment or complete text? How and why was an inference made?
2. What can we conclude from a passage or complete text? How and why was that conclusion met?

	Learning Goals	GED
Knowledge Goals:	1. Understand how to make inferences and draw conclusions.	R.2.3
	2. Compare and contrast inferences and conclusions.	R.2.8
Reading Goals:	1. Make inferences about supporting details.	R.2.3
	2. Draw conclusions or make generalizations based on the main ideas in a text.	R.2.8
Vocabulary Goals:	1. Define key subject and academic vocabulary.	R.4.1
	2. Determine the meaning of unknown vocabulary using context clues, word forms, and parts of speech.	
	3. Produce writing and speech using new vocabulary.	
Written Response Goals:	1. Determine what is stated in the text and make logical inferences or conclusions supported by text evidence.	W.1 W.2
	2. Respond to text by summarizing events clearly, organizing information logically, supporting conclusions with examples, and focusing on the writing task.	W.3
	3. Use standard English language conventions. *(See Language Usage Goals)*	
Language Usage Goals:	1. Identify the subject and predicate and the correct subject/predicate order.	L.1.5
	2. Edit writing to include complete sentences with the correct subject/predicate order.	L.1.6

Sample Instructional Support Strategies

> ## Bridging Knowledge

Strategy 1: *Develop prior knowledge and skills to connect to new knowledge.*
Strategy 2: *Use guiding questions to make connections beyond the lesson to broader life themes and topics.*
Strategy 3: *Use reading strategies to develop, monitor, and synthesize new knowledge.* *(See Bridging Reading)*
Strategy 4: *Demonstrate (and further develop) synthesis of new knowledge through written student response tasks.* *(See Bridging Written Response)*

1. Evaluate students' knowledge of the following language arts concepts and skills. Utilize the chart below to develop student background knowledge and skills as necessary.

Inferences and Conclusions	Reading Inferences Drawing Conclusions	Writing Summary Conclusions	Language Usage Subject/Predicates
Writing for the GED Test Book 1: Grammar, Usage, and Mechanics			Basic Sentence Parts (p. 20); Nouns and Personal Pronouns (p. 38); Verb Tenses and Forms (p. 42)
Core Skills in Reading & Writing	Unit 3, Lesson 4: Drawing Conclusions (p. 65); Lesson 6: Summarizing (p. 71)	Unit 5, Lesson 1: Topic Sentences (p. 115); Lesson 2: Supporting Details (p. 118); Lesson 3: Transitions (p. 121)	Unit 4: Lesson 1: Parts of Speech (p. 80); Lesson 2: Sentence Structure (p. 84)
Scoreboost: Writing Across the Tests Sentence Structure, Usage, and Mechanics (SS); Responding to Text (RT)		RT: Summarize Main Idea or Theme (p. 31) [Science related]	
Scoreboost: Thinking Skills Critical Thinking	Make Inferences (p. 8); Draw Conclusions (p. 20)	Summarize Ideas (p. 6); Draw Conclusions (p. 20)	
Pre-HSE Workbook Reading (R); Writing 1 (W1); Writing 2 (W2)	R: Inferences and Conclusions (p. 14)		W1: Parts of a Sentence (p. 12); Basic Verb Tenses & Forms (p. 24)

2. Contextualize the GED Application portion of the lesson (p. 10) within a broader theme or topic by beginning the lesson with Guiding Questions. Guiding questions that are authentic and relevant to students draw them deeper into the lesson and allow them to build deeper knowledge beyond the content of the lesson.

Guiding Questions: 1. What can you conclude from the text about settling the West in the 1800s? 2. How do the details of the text support your conclusion?

➤ Bridging Reading

> **Strategy 1:** *Determine the type of text, establish reading purpose, and make predictions using text features and signal words.*
>
> **Strategy 2:** *Develop text analysis using think-alouds, annotation, sentence frames, and graphic organizers.*
>
> **Strategy 3:** *Overcome text analysis barriers using prior knowledge, analyzing language usage, and using resources.*
>
> **Strategy 4:** *Synthesize text analysis using paraphrasing, text frames, graphic organizers, and peer discussions.*

1. Have students use pre-reading strategies (p. 8) to scan the text features and signal words to determine the type of text, its purpose, the purpose of the reading task (test prompt or question), and make predictions about the text. Given only a few obvious text features or clues, students may scan the first paragraph. A graphic organizer may be helpful for noting this information.

Example: Guided Practice (p. 8), *Silverspot: The Story of a Crow*

	Answer	**Text Features**	**Signal Words**
Text Type	Narrative	Title, dialogue	story
Text Purpose	Descriptive/informative	Title, first sentence	A question opens the story
Reading Purpose	Answer questions about inference	The questions in the margins	think, like, suggest, feel
Prediction	Will tell about a special crow	Title	"Story of a Crow"

2. The Guided Practice portion of the lesson utilizes annotation strategies and a graphic organizer to model the text analysis process students can use for the GED Application portion. However, additional annotations (in the margins or a notebook) are helpful: 1) underlining the topic sentence in the first paragraph and main ideas thereafter; 2) dissecting confusing words or passages; and 3) noting *who, where, when*, and *what/main idea* for each paragraph.

Example: Guided Practice, paragraph 3: Noting *who, where, when*, and *what/main idea*

Who: Silverspot, narrator
Where: on the bridge
When: on a windy day
What: Silverspot warns other crows

3. As the lesson explains, to make inferences and draw conclusions, having prior knowledge and experience is essential. This may be problematic for ELLs because first the theme/topic may be outside their realm of experience, and second, they may have difficulty understanding signal words due to unfamiliar vocabulary or complex sentence structure. Providing resources to bridge ELL's prior knowledge and language development will be helpful.

Prior-Knowledge Aids	**Language Aids**
images, analogies, other texts with related theme/topic, collaborative pre-reading activities to introduce the topic	target vocabulary for practice and word study *(See Bridging Vocabulary)*, sentence dissection, language usage resources, Language for Specific Purposes (p. 136).

4. Students can use their annotations to summarize each section of the text. Make sure they are paraphrasing the text. Using annotations of *who*, *where*, *when*, and *what* help students paraphrase as it takes them away from the exact wording and allows them to restate things in their own way. Here is an example summary of paragraph 3 in Guided Practice.

> The author was on the bridge when Silverspot and his group of crows flew over. Silverspot issued a warning to his group to be careful of the man on the bridge, so all the crows flew higher to avoid the man.

After students summarize each section of the text into one or two sentences, they can combine these sentences to create a summary paragraph. This is where the "signal words" they need to connect their ideas will bring cohesion to their writing.

> *Sequence:* first, second, next, then, after, since, prior to, during, finally
>
> *Example:* for example, such as, including, like, one example is, for instance
>
> *Summary:* in summary, to summarize, overall, to sum up, on the whole, in general

➤ Bridging Vocabulary

> **Strategy 1:** *Identify the component parts and usage of new words to interpret their meanings.*
>
> **Strategy 2:** *Use context clues to interpret new words, including figurative and connotative language.*
>
> **Strategy 3:** *Utilize vocabulary-building resources.*
>
> **Strategy 4:** *Build a deeper knowledge of words through writing and speaking tasks.*

1. First, present the shortest form of the word (the base word, often the verb form), followed by other commonly used word forms (if available). Examine prefixes and suffixes and their impact on word meaning and usage.

2. Read the word as used in the context of the text and discuss possible meanings given context clues and word form.

3. Have students find (electronically or in print) the definition or translation of the base form and, if different, the form used in context and note these definitions for future reference and study.

4. Gradually build a deeper knowledge of the word by having students use the word in a sentence frame, guided discussion, and an original sentence (see Appendix D, p. 144).

➤ Bridging Written Response

> **Strategy 1:** *Prepare for a response task by identifying its purpose, audience, signal words, structure, and style.*
>
> **Strategy 2:** *Organize text analysis for a written response using a graphic organizer and/or paragraph/essay frame.*
>
> **Strategy 3:** *Overcome barriers to producing clear/coherent writing by using models, language analysis, and resources.*
>
> **Strategy 4:** *Revise writing by utilizing peer- and self-editing checklists, rubrics, and writing resources.*
>
> **Strategy 5:** *Extend text analysis to build upon initial information or claims by using evidence from additional sources.*

1. To prepare for the response task, students need to identify the writing purpose (based on the writing prompt), the language they will use to meet their purpose (the signal words), and the area of language usage on which they will focus (Language Usage Goals). The graphic organizer below may help students with this preparation.

Task: Summarize the main events and information provided in the excerpt *Across the Plains in 1844* and draw conclusions about what it tells us about settling the West in the 1800s. Support your conclusions with examples from the text.

Text Type	Summary
Text Purpose	Summarize and conclude
Writing Purpose	Present conclusions drawn from the text about settling the West in the 1800s. Provide examples to support conclusion.
Signal Words	*Summary:* in summary, to summarize, overall, to sum up, on the whole, in general *Conclusions:* therefore, thus, in conclusion, as such, given, for this reason *Example:* for example, such as, including, like, one example is, for instance
Language Usage Goal	*Student chooses a language usage area on which to focus.*

2. Next students need to organize their ideas in a way that fits the conventions of the writing purpose. Since the excerpt is quite short, a paragraph or two will be sufficient for completing the task. There are a number of graphic organizers that can work for this step of the writing process. Here is one example:

Topic Sentence:					
Summary of events of the story			Conclusions about settling the West in the 1800s		
Event 1	Event 2	Event 3	Conclusion 1	Conclusion 2	Conclusion 3
Supporting Detail	Supporting Detail	Supporting Detail	Supporting Example	Supporting Example	Supporting Example
Conclusion:					

3. In Bridging Reading students completed a summary of the *Silverspot* excerpt. This provides a model for the summary portion of the written response task. Using this excerpt, model the second part of the task, presenting conclusions drawn from the text. For example, ask the question: "What conclusions could we draw from the *Silverspot* story about other animals in the animal kingdom?" Elicit ideas and compose, on the board with student help, conclusions supported by examples from the text.

4. Based on the area of language usage students have chosen to target, provide resources to help them revise their writing. At first, this may require the teacher to identify the problem area. However, with consistent exposure to self and peer editing, students should be able to identify such areas in their own and their peers' writing.

5. Provide students access to additional resources on settling the West in the 1800s. Guide them in similar bridging activities to analyze and synthesize each resource. Finally, support them in synthesizing the multiple resources into one essay by following Bridging Written Response strategies 1–4.

➢ **Bridging Language Usage**

> **Strategy 1:** *Determine and target areas of language usage that require further development.*
>
> **Strategy 2:** *Analyze specific areas of language usage as modeled in authentic and relevant communication tasks.*
>
> **Strategy 3:** *Develop specific areas of language usage through participation in authentic communication tasks.*
>
> **Strategy 4:** *Revise language usage by utilizing peer- and self-editing checklists, rubrics, and language resources.*

1. Determine the language needs of the students and choose a particular language usage area to focus on for this lesson. As an example, let's focus on *Writing* book 1, Basic Sentence Parts (p. 20).

2. Beginning with the reading (the context/the whole), focus on a problematic area of language usage (the parts) from the reading passage. Here is an example of how language usage analysis may work for this lesson.

> Bridging Reading Strategy 3 helps students overcome confusion with a particular sentence. They might dissect a sentence and reveal that they do not understand how to identify the main subject and predicate of the sentence. On the next day, remind students of the problematic sentence (the whole) and provide a "just-in-time" mini-lesson on subject and predicate identification (the parts). Have students practice by using the Basic Sentence Parts lesson from *Writing* book 1. Then, direct them back to the text to practice with sentences in the text. Using a quick visual assessment (thumbs up, sideways, or down, for example) see who needs to focus further on this area. Those students should then highlight this goal on their Language Usage Checklist (p. 129).

3. As mentioned in Strategy 2, students need to return to a contextualized communicative activity (the whole) to apply their analysis. Here's how it may look for this lesson:

> During follow-up writing activities (whether the synthesis portion of Bridging Reading or the Bridging Written Response activity), direct students to their Language Usage Checklist to choose their language usage goal. Students can target this language usage goal in their writing and editing. After writing is complete, students can self-assess (or the teacher may step in to do this for students who are less experienced with self-assessment), check off this goal if mastered, or revisit it during the next writing task.

4. To revise problematic areas of usage, students can use peer editing. Here is an example of how this may look in this lesson given the language usage goal of identifying and using subject and predicates.

> During the written response task, students can peer edit for inclusion of subject and predicate in all sentences using the Editing Rubric (p. 131). They should identify the subject and predicate in each sentence and circle any problem areas. Ask them to make suggestions on how to correct these areas. They might continue through the checklist to evaluate other areas of language usage, but do not specifically identify these or offer suggestions. However, once the initial problem area has been revised, another area may be targeted. Have students meet, share feedback, and revise their writing. Pay attention to supporting constructive peer conversations (see Discourse Prompts, p. 136).

➢ **Assessment & Next Steps**

Students should complete the suggested practice activities and the activities included in each lesson. Evaluate which learning goals were not met and remediate by using other resources, such as those identified in the Bridging Knowledge section. Upon successful completion, continue to the next lesson.

MAIN IDEAS AND SUPPORTING DETAILS

Skills-Based Questions

1. What is the overall main idea of the text and the main ideas that support it?

2. Which details in the text support each main idea and which kind of details are they?

	Learning Goals:	**GED**
Knowledge Goals:	1. Describe the relationship between the overall main idea and the "mini" main ideas that support it.	R.2.1
		R.2.5
	2. Describe what kinds of supporting details there are and give examples of each.	
Reading Goals:	1. Identify and comprehend main ideas and details in text.	R.2.1
	2. Identify which details support the main idea.	R.2.5
	3. Infer main ideas of texts and support with text evidence.	R.2.4
Vocabulary Goals:	1. Define key subject and academic vocabulary.	R.4.1
	2. Determine the meaning of unknown vocabulary using context clues, word forms, and parts of speech.	
	3. Produce writing and speech using new vocabulary.	
Written Response Goals:	1. Determine the main ideas of the text and the details that support them.	W.1
	2. Respond to text by summarizing information clearly, organizing information logically, and focusing on the writing task.	W.2
		W.3
	3. Use standard English language conventions. *(See Language Usage Goals)*	
Language Usage Goals:	1. Identify simple and compound sentences and use them correctly in writing.	L.1.6
	2. Edit writing to include compound sentences with appropriate conjunctions.	L.2.2

Sample Instructional Support Strategies

➢ **Bridging Knowledge**

> **Strategy 1:** *Develop prior knowledge and skills to connect to new knowledge.*
>
> **Strategy 2:** *Use guiding questions to make connections beyond the lesson to broader life themes and topics.*
>
> **Strategy 3:** *Use reading strategies to develop, monitor, and synthesize new knowledge.* (See Bridging Reading)
>
> **Strategy 4:** *Demonstrate (and further develop) synthesis of new knowledge through written student response tasks.* (See Bridging Written Response)

1. Evaluate students' knowledge of the following language arts concepts and skills. Utilize the chart below to develop student background knowledge and skills as necessary.

Main Ideas and Supporting Details	Reading Main Idea Supporting Details	Writing Summary Examples	Language Usage Simple and Compound Sentences; Subject-Verb Agreement
Writing for the GED Test Book 1: Grammar, Usage, and Mechanics			Simple and Compound Sentences (p. 22); Irregular Verbs (p. 44); Subject-Verb Agreement I (p. 48)
Core Skills in Reading & Writing	Unit 3, Lesson 2: Main Idea and Supporting Details (p. 59); Lesson 6: Summarizing (p. 71)	Unit 5, Lessons 1: Topic Sentences (p. 115); Lesson 2: Supporting Details (p. 118); Lesson 3: Transitions (p. 121)	Unit 4, Lesson 2: Sentence Structure (p. 84); Lesson 3: Types of Sentences (p. 88)
Scoreboost: Writing Across the Tests Sentence Structure, Usage, and Mechanics (SS); Responding to Text (RT)		RT: Summarize Main Idea or Theme (p. 31); Identify Specific Details in Text (p. 33) [Science related]	SS: Make Subjects and Verbs Agree (p. 20)
Scoreboost: Thinking Skills Critical Thinking			
Pre-HSE Workbook Reading (R); Writing 1 (W1); Writing 2 (W2)	R: Main Idea (p. 20); Supporting Details (p. 22)		W1: Compound Sentences (p. 36); Subject-Verb Agreement (p. 30)

2. Contextualize the GED Application portion of the lesson (p. 16) within a broader theme or topic by beginning the lesson with Guiding Questions. Guiding questions that are authentic and relevant to students draw them deeper into the lesson and allow them to build deeper knowledge beyond the content of the lesson.

> **Guiding Questions:**
>
> 1. What is the main idea of the passage *An Ongoing Global Issue*, and what details in the text support it?
>
> 2. What other local, regional, national or global examples could you offer in support of this main idea?

> **Bridging Reading**

Strategy 1: Determine the type of text, establish reading purpose, and make predictions using text features and signal words.

Strategy 2: Develop text analysis using think-alouds, annotation, sentence frames, and graphic organizers.

Strategy 3: Overcome text analysis barriers using prior knowledge, analyzing language usage, and using resources.

Strategy 4: Synthesize text analysis using paraphrasing, text frames, graphic organizers, and peer discussions.

1. Have students use pre-reading strategies (p. 8) to scan the text features and signal words to determine the type of text, its purpose, the purpose of the reading task (test prompt or question), and make predictions about the text. Given only a few obvious text features or clues, students may scan the first paragraph. A graphic organizer may be helpful for noting this information.

Example: Guided Practice (p. 14), *Living Together*

	Answers	**Text Features**	**Signal Words**
Text Type	Informational	Headings, vocabulary in italics	Science words: symbiosis, mutualism, etc.
Text Purpose	Informative	Same as above	Same as above
Reading Purpose	Answer questions about main idea and details	The directions; the questions in margins	In questions: main idea, details
Prediction	To tell about animals that live together	Title, headings, second sentence in the intro	"Living together," rhinoceros, bird

2. The Guided Practice portion of the lesson utilizes annotation strategies and a graphic organizer to model the text analysis process students can use for the GED Application portion. However, additional annotations (in the margins or a notebook) are helpful: 1) underlining the topic sentence in the first paragraph and main ideas thereafter; 2) dissecting confusing words or passages; and 3) noting *who*, *where*, *when*, and *what*/*main idea* for each paragraph.

Example: Guided Practice: Underlining the topic sentence and main ideas

Intro: <u>Symbiotic relationships can be divided into three categories: mutualism, commensalism, and parasitism.</u>

Paragraph 2: <u>In mutualistic relationships, each species provides a benefit to the other that helps both species' chances of survival.</u>

3. Choosing the main idea and supporting details involves understanding hierarchical relationships. Along with language challenges, ELLs—especially those with limited and/or interrupted education—may struggle with abstract concepts. Using basic examples from everyday life is a powerful way to make the connections. Give several examples of common hierarchical relationships and then have students pair up to create and share their own. Try doing this by using a simple graphic organizer with a common example as an analogy for the main idea and supporting details. The following graphic organizers show the hierarchy relationship of a broad topic (the main idea) at the top supported by many pieces that fall under that topic (the supporting details).

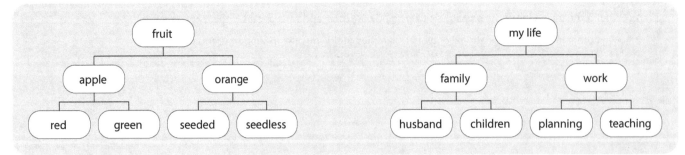

4. Students can use the main ideas and details they identified (underlined) in their annotations to fill in a graphic organizer with information from the text.

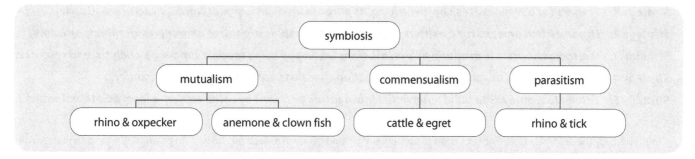

After students develop a graphic organizer, they can create a summary paragraph. Here is where they use "signal words" to connect their ideas and bring cohesion to their writing.

Definition: is defined as, means, is called, referred to as

Sequence: first, second, next, then, after, since, prior to, during, finally

Example: for example, such as, including, like, one example is, for instance

➢ Bridging Vocabulary

Strategy 1: *Identify the component parts and usage of new words to interpret their meanings.*

Strategy 2: *Use context clues to interpret new words, including figurative and connotative language.*

Strategy 3: *Utilize vocabulary-building resources.*

Strategy 4: *Build a deeper knowledge of words through writing and speaking tasks.*

1. First, present the shortest form of the word (the base word, often the verb form), followed by other commonly used word forms (if available). Examine prefixes and suffixes and their impact on word meaning and usage.

2. Read the word as used in the context of the text and discuss possible meanings given context clues and word form.

3. Have students find (electronically or in print) the definition or translation of the base form and, if different, the form used in context and note these definitions for future reference and study.

4. Gradually build a deeper knowledge of the word by having students use the word in a sentence frame, guided discussion, and an original sentence (see Appendix D, p. 144).

➤ **Bridging Written Response**

> **Strategy 1:** Prepare for a response task by identifying its purpose, audience, signal words, structure, and style.
>
> **Strategy 2:** Organize text analysis for a written response using a graphic organizer and/or paragraph/essay frame.
>
> **Strategy 3:** Overcome barriers to producing clear/coherent writing by using models, language analysis, and resources.
>
> **Strategy 4:** Revise writing by utilizing peer- and self-editing checklists, rubrics, and writing resources.
>
> **Strategy 5:** Extend text analysis to build upon initial information or claims by using evidence from additional sources.

1. To prepare for the response task, students need to identify the writing purpose (based on the writing prompt), the language they will use to meet their purpose (the signal words), and the area of language usage on which they will focus (Language Usage Goal). The graphic organizer below may help students with this preparation.

Task: Summarize the information provided in the passage *An Ongoing Global Issue* and provide an additional example of desertification happening on the planet now or recently.

Text Type	Summary
Text Purpose	Summarize and apply to another example
Writing Purpose	Summarize main information and provide another example of desertification.
Signal Words	*Summary:* in summary, to summarize, overall, to sum up, on the whole, in general *Example:* for example, such as, including, like, one example is, for instance *Cause/effect:* due to, since, in order to, because of, therefore, consequently, as a result
Language Usage Goal	*Student chooses a language usage area on which to focus.*

2. Next, students need to organize their ideas in a way that fits the conventions of the writing purpose. Since the passage is quite short, a paragraph or two will be sufficient for completing the task. Students can use the same graphic organizer they used above or the one from the previous lesson.

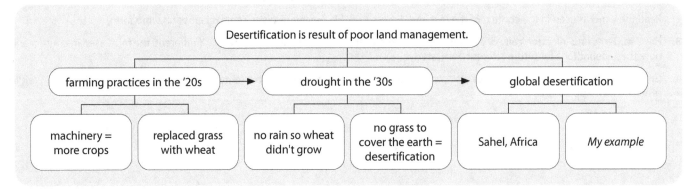

3. In Bridging Reading students completed a summary of the *Living Together* passage. This provides a model for the summary portion of the written response task. Using this passage, model the second part of the task, presenting another example of symbiosis from research or prior knowledge. For example, ask the question: "What other examples of symbiosis do you know about?" Elicit ideas and compose, on the board with student help, information about one additional example.

4. Based on the area of language usage students have chosen to target, provide resources to help them revise their writing. At first, this may require the teacher to identify the problem area. However, with consistent exposure to self and peer editing, students should be able to identify such areas in their own and their peers' writing.

5. Provide students access to additional resources on global problems with desertification. Guide them in similar bridging activities to analyze and synthesize each resource. Finally, support them in synthesizing the multiple resources into one essay by following Bridging Written Response strategies 1–4.

➤ **Bridging Language Usage**

> *Strategy 1:* Determine and target areas of language usage that require further development.
>
> *Strategy 2:* Analyze specific areas of language usage as modeled in authentic and relevant communication tasks.
>
> *Strategy 3:* Develop specific areas of language usage through participation in authentic communication tasks.
>
> *Strategy 4:* Revise language usage by utilizing peer- and self-editing checklists, rubrics, and language resources.

1. Determine the language needs of the students and choose a particular language usage area to focus on for this lesson. As an example, let's focus on *Writing* book 1, Simple and Compound Sentences (p. 22).

2. Beginning with the reading (the context/the whole), focus on a problematic area of language usage (the parts) from the reading passage. Here is an example of how language usage analysis may work for this lesson.

> Bridging Reading Strategy 3 helps students overcome confusion with a particular sentence. The sentence is a compound sentence that students only understood once it was broken into two segments. On the next day, remind students of this compound sentence and provide a "just-in-time" mini-lesson using the Simple and Compound Sentences lesson from *Writing* book 1. Then, direct students to practice dissecting other compound sentences from the text. For a quick assessment, ask students to take two simple sentences from the text and create a compound sentence on a slip of paper and evaluate what they have written. Students who need more practice in this area should highlight this goal on their Language Usage Checklist (p. 129).

3. As mentioned in Strategy 2, students need to return to a contextualized communicative activity (the whole) to apply their analysis. Here's how it may look for this lesson:

> During follow-up writing activities (whether the synthesis portion of Bridging Reading or the Bridging Written Response activity), direct students to their Language Usage Checklist to choose their language usage goal. Students can target this language usage goal in their writing and editing. After writing is complete, students can self-assess (or the teacher may step in to do this for students who are less experienced with self-assessment), check off this goal if mastered, or revisit it during the next writing task.

4. To revise problematic areas of usage, students can use peer editing. Here is an example of how this may look in this lesson given the language usage goal of identifying and using simple and compound sentences.

> During the written response task, students can peer edit for inclusion of correct simple and compound sentences using the Editing Rubric (p. 131). They identify the subject, predicate, and coordinating conjunction (if any) in each sentence and circle any problem areas. Ask them to make suggestions on how to correct these areas. They might continue through the checklist to evaluate other areas of language usage, but do not specifically identify these or offer suggestions. Have students meet, share feedback, and revise their writing. Pay attention to supporting constructive peer conversations (see Discourse Prompts, p. 136).

➤ **Assessment & Next Steps**

Students should complete the suggested practice activities and the activities included in each lesson. Evaluate which learning goals were not met and remediate by using other resources, such as those identified in the Bridging Knowledge section. Upon successful completion, continue to the next lesson.

SEQUENCE OF EVENTS

Skills-Based Questions

1. What kinds of texts use sequential order?

2. How is sequential order, including chronological order, used in texts?

	Learning Goals	GED
Knowledge Goals:	1. Determine the main ideas and supporting details of a text.	R.2.1
	2. Describe the sequence of events or steps in a text.	R.3.1
Reading Goals:	1. Identify and comprehend main idea and details in text.	R.2.1
	2. Determine the sequence of events in texts.	R.3.1
	3. Identify signal words that show sequence in the text.	R.5.3
Vocabulary Goals:	1. Define key subject and academic vocabulary.	R.4.1
	2. Determine the meaning of unknown vocabulary using context clues, word forms, and parts of speech.	
	3. Produce writing and speech using new vocabulary.	
Written Response Goals:	1. Determine the main ideas of the text and the details that support them.	W.1
	2. Respond to text by summarizing information clearly, organizing information sequentially, and focusing on the writing task.	W.2 W.3
	3. Use standard English language conventions. *(See Language Usage Goals)*	
Language Usage Goals:	1. Identify complex sentences and use them correctly in writing.	L.1.6
	2. Identify and correct errors in subject-verb agreement.	L.1.2
	3. Edit writing to include complex sentences with appropriate transition words and punctuation.	L.2.2 L.1.9

Sample Instructional Support Strategies

> ### Bridging Knowledge

Strategy 1: *Develop prior knowledge and skills to connect to new knowledge.*

Strategy 2: *Use guiding questions to make connections beyond the lesson to broader life themes and topics.*

Strategy 3: *Use reading strategies to develop, monitor, and synthesize new knowledge.* (See Bridging Reading)

Strategy 4: *Demonstrate (and further develop) synthesis of new knowledge through written student response tasks.* (See Bridging Written Response)

1. Evaluate students' knowledge of the following language arts concepts and skills. Utilize the chart below to develop student background knowledge and skills as necessary.

Sequence of Events	Reading Sequencing	Writing Summary Sequencing	Language Usage Complex Sentences Subject-Verb Agreement
Writing for the GED Test Book 1: Grammar, Usage, and Mechanics			Complex Sentences (p. 24); The Perfect Tenses (p. 46); Subject-Verb Agreement II (p. 50); Commas (p. 66)
Core Skills in Reading & Writing	Unit 3, Lesson 3: Text Structure (p. 62)	Unit 3, Lesson 6: Summarizing (p. 71) Unit 5, Lessons 1: Topic Sentences (p. 115); Lesson 2: Supporting Details (p. 118); Lesson 3: Transitions (p. 121)	Unit 4, Lesson 3: Types of Sentences (p. 88); Lesson 4: Commas (p. 92); Lesson 6: Agreement (p. 99)
Scoreboost: Writing Across the Tests Sentence Structure, Usage, and Mechanics (SS); Responding to Text (RT)		RT: Organize Supporting Ideas (p. 12)	SS: Coordinate Ideas in Sentences (p. 6); Subordinate Ideas in Sentences (p. 8); Make Subjects and Verbs Agree (p. 20); Use Commas Correctly (p. 32)
Scoreboost: Thinking Skills Critical Thinking	Follow a Sequence (p. 16)	Summarize Ideas (p. 6)	
Pre-HSE Workbook Reading (R); Writing 1 (W1); Writing 2 (W2)		W2: Order of Ideas (p. 20)	W1: Complex Sentences (p. 38); Irregular Verbs (p. 26); Subject-Verb Agreement (p. 30)

2. Contextualize the GED Application portion of the lesson (p. 22) within a broader theme or topic by beginning the lesson with Guiding Questions. Guiding questions that are authentic and relevant to students draw them deeper into the lesson and allow them to build deeper knowledge beyond the content of the lesson.

> **Guiding Questions:**
>
> 1. Why did Lewis and Clark explore the lands west of the Mississippi and what happened on this expedition?
>
> 2. Based on your knowledge of U.S. history, what events in the 1800s did this expedition trigger?

➢ **Bridging Reading**

Strategy 1: *Determine the type of text, establish reading purpose, and make predictions using text features and signal words.*

Strategy 2: *Develop text analysis using think-alouds, annotation, sentence frames, and graphic organizers.*

Strategy 3: *Overcome text analysis barriers using prior knowledge, analyzing language usage, and using resources.*

Strategy 4: *Synthesize text analysis using paraphrasing, text frames, graphic organizers, and peer discussions.*

1. Have students scan the text features and signal words to determine the type of text, its purpose, the purpose of the reading task (test prompt or question), and make predictions about the text. Given just a few obvious text features or clues, students may scan the first paragraph. A graphic organizer may be helpful for noting this information.

Example: Guided Practice (p. 20), *The Science of Sleep*

	Answers	Text Features	Signal Words
Text Type	Informational	Title	science, stages
Text Purpose	Informative about process	Same as above	Same as above
Reading Purpose	Answer questions about main idea and sequence	The directions, the questions in margins	In questions: main idea, sequence, first stage
Prediction	Will tell about the stages of sleep	Title, the questions in margins	first stage, new stage

2. The Guided Practice portion of the lesson utilizes annotation strategies and a graphic organizer to model the text analysis process students can use for the GED Application portion. Aside from the practice activity in the lesson, the graphic organizer can be used as an annotation tool to develop understanding of each paragraph of the text.

Example, Guided Practice, paragraph 2:

Stage 1	Stage 2	Stage 3	Stage 4
5–10 minutes Flaccid paralysis	Brain waves slow No conscious awareness	Brain has 20% delta waves Deepest sleep	Eyes move side-to-side Dream state

3. Although sequencing may seem like a basic concept, there are cultures that have more fluid interpretations of processes and do not use a rigid sequential order to tell narratives or to describe a process. Providing relevant examples for learners on the importance of sequential order in American culture is helpful. Imagine the confusion if the sequence of events in the following situations was told in this order.

Filing an Accident Report	Work Instructions	Drawing Blood
The car hit me. I drove through the intersection. The light turned green.	Shut down the cash register. Count the cash in the register. Lock the doors to the store.	Stick the needle in the arm. Wash the area of entry. Choose a vein to enter.

4. Students can use the details they noted in the graphic organizer to summarize each stage of the sleep process. Use a paragraph frame to guide them. Make sure they focus on the signal words for sequencing (p. 19 in the lesson has an excellent list of these words).

➤ Bridging Vocabulary

Strategy 1: **Identify the component parts and usage of new words to interpret their meanings.**

Strategy 2: **Use context clues to interpret new words, including figurative and connotative language.**

Strategy 3: **Utilize vocabulary-building resources.**

Strategy 4: **Build a deeper knowledge of words through writing and speaking tasks.**

1. First, present the shortest form of the word (the base word, often the verb form), followed by other commonly used word forms (if available). Examine prefixes and suffixes and their impact on word meaning and usage.

2. Read the word as used in the context of the text and discuss possible meanings given context clues and word form.

3. Have students find (electronically or in print) the definition or translation of the base form and, if different, the form used in context and note these definitions for future reference and study.

4. Gradually build a deeper knowledge of the word by having students use the word in a sentence frame, guided discussion, and an original sentence (see Appendix D, p. 144).

➤ **Bridging Written Response**

Strategy 1: *Prepare for a response task by identifying its purpose, audience, signal words, structure, and style.*

Strategy 2: *Organize text analysis for a written response using a graphic organizer and/or paragraph/essay frame.*

Strategy 3: *Overcome barriers to producing clear/coherent writing by using models, language analysis, and resources.*

Strategy 4: *Revise writing by utilizing peer- and self-editing checklists, rubrics, and writing resources.*

Strategy 5: *Extend text analysis to build upon initial information or claims by using evidence from additional sources.*

---

1. To prepare for the response task, students need to identify the writing purpose (based on the writing prompt), the language they will use to meet their purpose (the signal words), and the area of language usage on which they will focus (Language Usage Goals). The graphic organizer below may help students with this preparation.

Task: Summarize in chronological order the events of the Lewis and Clark expedition. Then, provide additional information on two or three historical events that this expedition triggered.

Text Type	Summary and informational
Text Purpose	Summarize and expand
Writing Purpose	Summarize events in time order and describe other events that happened after
Signal Words	*Summary:* in summary, to summarize, overall, to sum up, on the whole, in general *Sequence:* first, second, next, then, after, since, prior to, during, finally
Language Usage Goal	*Student chooses a language usage area on which to focus.*

2. Next students need to organize their ideas in a way that fits the conventions of the writing purpose. Since the passage is quite short, a paragraph or two will be sufficient for completing the task. Students can create a timeline (a skill required for the GED) to chronologically organize the events and add subsequent ones. To build this skill, separate students into groups and have them write each event on a note card and then put the note cards in order. Next, have them disperse the note cards in a zigzag fashion on either side of a yardstick or string. When they are sure they have the right order, students can transfer the timeline to paper.

1803: Jefferson made the Louisiana Purchase	Took Missouri River north	Sept. 11, 1805: began trek through Bitterroot Mtns.	Sept. 15: Found trail and made it 12 miles	Ate horses, almost starved

1804: Lewis and Clark Expedition began	Crossed the country to Idaho and Montana	Sept. 14: Bad weather, lost the trail	Sept. 16: Snow began and didn't stop	Sept. 22: reached end of Bitterroots

3. In Bridging Reading students completed a summary of the *Science of Sleep* passage. This provides a model for the summary portion of the written response task. Using the *Lewis and Clark* excerpt, model the second part of the task, which requires students to "provide additional information on two or three historical event that this expedition triggered." For example, ask the question: "What other historical events do you know about that followed this expedition?" Elicit ideas about one additional event and add it to the timeline. Together, create a summary sentence of the event.

4. Based on the area of language usage students have chosen to target, provide resources to help them revise their writing. At first, this may require the teacher to identify the problem area. However, with consistent exposure to self and peer editing, students should be able to identify such areas in their own and their peers' writing.

5. Provide students access to additional resources on historical events after Lewis and Clark's "gateway" expedition. Guide them in summarizing two or three important events. Students can then add these events to the timeline and their written response.

➢ Bridging Language Usage

> **Strategy 1:** Determine and target areas of language usage that require further development.
>
> **Strategy 2:** Analyze specific areas of language usage as modeled in authentic and relevant communication tasks.
>
> **Strategy 3:** Develop specific areas of language usage through participation in authentic communication tasks.
>
> **Strategy 4:** Revise language usage by utilizing peer- and self-editing checklists, rubrics, and language resources.

1. Determine the language needs of the students and choose a particular language usage area to focus on for this lesson. As an example, let's focus on *Writing* book 1, Complex Sentences (p. 24).

2. Beginning with the reading (the context/the whole), focus on a problematic area of language usage (the parts) from the reading passage. A focus on sequencing provides the opportunity for students to identify (and create) complex sentences using time clauses. First, students can complete the practice activities in the *Writing* book 1, Complex Sentences lesson. Then students can return to the text and scan for sequencing signal words and the phrases and/or clauses that follow. They should categorize these as prepositional phrases or clauses and annotate the signal word, subject, and verb. This graphic organizer may help with this.

Prepositional Phrases	Clauses
Circle signal word	Circle signal word, underline subject once & verb twice
(Before) 1803,	(When) they camped,

3. As mentioned in Strategy 2, students need to return to a contextualized communicative activity (the whole) to apply their analysis. Students can include time clauses in their written response activities using the sentences they pulled from the text as models. Here is an example of some time clauses they may create.

> After Lewis and Clark took the Missouri River north, _____.
>
> When they entered the Bitterroot Mountains, _____.
>
> Before they made it through the Bitterroots, _____..

4. To revise problematic areas of usage, students can use peer editing.

   Students peer edit for inclusion of complex sentences using the Editing Rubric (p. 131). They should identify the signal word, subject, and verb in each time clause and circle any problem areas. Ask them to make suggestions on how to correct these areas. They might continue through the checklist to evaluate other areas of language usage as well, but do not specifically identify these or offer suggestions. Have students meet, share feedback, and revise their writing. Pay attention to supporting constructive peer conversations (see Discourse Prompts, p. 136).

> (After) Lewis and Clark took the Missouri River north, they crossed the plains to Idaho and Montana.
>
> (When) entered the Bitterroot Mountains, the weather was getting cold.

No subject.
Add "they."

➢ Assessment & Next Steps

Students should complete the suggested practice activities and the activities included in each lesson. Evaluate which learning goals were not met and remediate by using other resources, such as those identified in the Bridging Knowledge section. Upon successful completion, continue to the next lesson.

COMPARISONS AND CONTRASTS

Skills-Based Questions

1. How do we compare and contrast different pieces of information in a text?
2. How is an author's message supported through comparing and contrasting?

	Learning Goals:	**GED**
Knowledge Goals:	1. Compare and contrast elements of the content of a text.	R.3.3
Reading Goals:	1. Compare and contrast the main subjects or events of the text.	R.3.3
	2. Make inferences about relationships between ideas in a text, such as compare and contrast.	R.3.4
	3. Identify signal words that show compare and contrast in the text.	R.5.3
Vocabulary Goals:	1. Define key subject and academic vocabulary.	R.4.1
	2. Determine the meaning of unknown vocabulary using context clues, word forms, and parts of speech.	
	3. Produce writing and speech using new vocabulary.	
Written Response Goals:	1. Use main ideas and text details to compare and contrast.	W.1
	2. Respond to text by comparing and contrasting information from the text, organizing the text to support this, and focusing on the writing task.	W.2
		W.3
	3. Use standard English language conventions. *(See Language Usage Goals)*	
Language Usage Goals:	1. Identify simple, compound, and complex sentences and use them correctly in writing.	L.1.6
	2. Identify and correct errors in complex subject-verb agreement.	L.1.7
	3. Edit writing to include a variety of sentence structures with appropriate transition words and punctuation.	L.2.2
		L.1.9

Sample Instructional Support Strategies

➢ **Bridging Knowledge**

> *Strategy 1:* **Develop prior knowledge and skills to connect to new knowledge.**
>
> *Strategy 2:* **Use guiding questions to make connections beyond the lesson to broader life themes and topics.**
>
> *Strategy 3:* **Use reading strategies to develop, monitor, and synthesize new knowledge.** *(See Bridging Reading)*
>
> *Strategy 4:* **Demonstrate (and further develop) synthesis of new knowledge through written student response tasks.** *(See Bridging Written Response)*

1. Evaluate students' knowledge of the following language arts concepts and skills. Utilize the chart below to develop student background knowledge and skills as necessary.

Comparisons and Contrasts	Reading Compare and Contrast	Writing Compare and Contrast	Language Usage Varied Sentence Structure Subject-Verb Agreement
Writing for the GED Test Book 1: Grammar, Usage, and Mechanics			Simple and Compound Sentences (p. 22); Complex Sentences (p. 24); Other Kinds of Pronouns (p. 40); Subject-Verb Agreement II (p. 50); Commas (p. 66)
Core Skills in Reading & Writing	Unit 3, Lesson 3: Text Structure (p. 62)	Unit 5, Lessons 1: Topic Sentences (p. 115); Lesson 2: Supporting Details (p. 118); Lesson 3: Transitions (p. 121) Unit 6, Lesson 1: Types of Essays (p. 125)	Unit 4, Lesson 3: Types of Sentences (p. 88); Lesson 4: Commas (p. 92); Lesson 6: Agreement (p. 99)
Scoreboost: Writing Across the Tests Sentence Structure, Usage, and Mechanics (SS); Responding to Text (RT)			SS: Coordinate Ideas in Sentences (p. 6); Subordinate Ideas in Sentences (p. 8); Make Subjects and Verbs Agree in Complicated Sentence Structures (p. 22)
Scoreboost: Thinking Skills Critical Thinking	Compare and Contrast Ideas (p. 28)	Compare and Contrast Ideas (p. 28)	
Pre-HSE Workbook Reading (R); Writing 1 (W1); Writing 2 (W2)	R: Compare and Contrast (p. 26)	W2: Order of Ideas (p. 20)	W1: Complete Sentences (p. 34); Compound Sentences (p. 36); Complex Sentences (p. 38)

2. Contextualize the GED Application portion of the lesson (p. 28) within a broader theme or topic by beginning the lesson with Guiding Questions. Guiding questions that are authentic and relevant to students draw them deeper into the lesson and allow them to build deeper knowledge beyond the content of the lesson.

> **Guiding Questions:**
>
> 1. How did Herbert Hoover and Franklin D. Roosevelt's responses to the Great Depression differ, and what was the result of their different reactions?
>
> 2. How was FDR's response to the Great Depression similar and/or different from Obama's response to the Great Recession?

> **Bridging Reading**

Strategy 1: *Determine the type of text, establish reading purpose, and make predictions using text features and signal words.*

Strategy 2: *Develop text analysis using think-alouds, annotation, sentence frames, and graphic organizers.*

Strategy 3: *Overcome text analysis barriers using prior knowledge, analyzing language usage, and using resources.*

Strategy 4: *Synthesize text analysis using paraphrasing, text frames, graphic organizers, and peer discussions.*

1. Have students use pre-reading strategies (p. 8) to scan the text features and signal words to determine the type of text, its purpose, the purpose of the reading task (test prompt or question), and make predictions about the text. Given only a few obvious text features or clues, students may scan the first paragraph. A graphic organizer may be helpful for noting this information.

Example: Guided Practice (p. 26), *Booker T. Washington and W. E. B. Du Bois*

	Answers	**Text Features**	**Signal Words**
Text Type	Informational	Title	
Text Purpose	Informative: Compare/contrast	Title, the questions in the margins, Venn diagram	In the questions: different from, two differences
Reading Purpose	Answer questions about main idea and contrasts	Directions, the questions in margins	Same as above
Prediction	Will tell how Booker T. Washington and W.E.B. Du Bois differ on civil rights approaches	Title, the questions in margins	Same as above

2. The Guided Practice portion of the lesson utilizes annotation strategies and a graphic organizer to model the text analysis process students can use for the GED Application portion. However, to aid students with their annotations as they develop their understanding of each section of the text, a simple T-chart can help outline and connect important information for each individual to compare and contrast. Later, students can apply this information to the Venn diagram in the lesson.

Important Points

Booker T. Washington	**W. E. B Du Bois**
Born in slavery, in 1856	Born free in 1868
Learned to read/write and became a teacher	Went to school as a child, got Ph.D.
Believed in financial independence for African Americans through education	Believed in political action and protest
Believed education in trades was best route	Believed in education
He was an accommodationist	Believed in liberal arts education over trades

3. The language signaling compare and contrast is very distinct. Students can find a list of these signal words listed at the bottom of page 24 of the Comparisons and Contrasts lesson. Other signal words will include nouns and verbs that show similarity or difference (agree/agreement: concur; oppose/opposition: differ/difference) and negatives (not, none, any). Providing a reference list of these words for ELLs is very helpful in both reading analysis and writing.

4. Using the details they noted in the T-chart, students can populate the Venn diagram in the lesson. Using a paragraph frame, such as the one below, they can then write a summary paragraph that compares and contrasts this information. Students can use either the Block or the Point-by-Point system described in the Comparisons and Contrasts lesson (p. 25). Make sure students focus on the signal words for compare and contrast.

Block	Point-by-Point
[Topic Sentence] _(first subject)_ and _(second subject)_ have _(introduce that you will compare and contrast the two subjects here)_ . _(First subject)_ was _(point 1)_ . He _(point 2)_ . **In addition,** he _(point 3)_ . **Furthermore,** he _(point 4)_ . _(Second subject)_ , **on the other hand,** was _(point 1)_ . **Unlike** _(subject 1)_ , he _(point 2)_ . **Furthermore,** he _(point 3)_ . **Another difference** was that he _(point 4)_ . [Conclusion] **Although both** _(general similarity)_ , _(general difference)_ .	[Topic Sentence] _(first subject)_ and _(second subject)_ have _(introduce that you will compare and contrast the two subjects here)_ . _(First subject-point 1)_ . **However,** _(second subject-point 1)_ . **Although** _(first subject-point 2)_ , _(second subject-point 2)_ . _(First subject-point 3)_ . **On the other hand,** _(second subject-point 3)_ . The **greatest difference** between the two men was _(point 4)_ . [Conclusion] **Although both** _(general similarity)_ , _(general difference)_ .

> ## Bridging Vocabulary

Strategy 1: *Identify the component parts and usage of new words to interpret their meanings.*

Strategy 2: *Use context clues to interpret new words, including figurative and connotative language.*

Strategy 3: *Utilize vocabulary-building resources.*

Strategy 4: *Build a deeper knowledge of words through writing and speaking tasks.*

1. First, present the shortest form of the word (the base word, often the verb form), followed by other commonly used word forms (if available). Examine prefixes and suffixes and their impact on word meaning and usage.

2. Read the word as used in the context of the text and discuss possible meanings given context clues and word form.

3. Have students find (electronically or in print) the definition or translation of the base form and, if different, the form used in context and note these definitions for future reference and study.

4. Gradually build a deeper knowledge of the word by having students use the word in a sentence frame, guided discussion, and an original sentence (see Appendix D, p. 144).

➢ Bridging Written Response

Strategy 1: *Prepare for a response task by identifying its purpose, audience, signal words, structure, and style.*

Strategy 2: *Organize text analysis for a written response using a graphic organizer and/or paragraph/essay frame.*

Strategy 3: *Overcome barriers to producing clear/coherent writing by using models, language analysis, and resources.*

Strategy 4: *Revise writing by utilizing peer- and self-editing checklists, rubrics, and writing resources.*

Strategy 5: *Extend text analysis to build upon initial information or claims by using evidence from additional sources.*

1. To prepare for the response task, students need to identify the writing purpose (based on the writing prompt), the language they will use to meet their purpose (the signal words), and the area of language usage on which they will focus (Language Usage Goals). The graphic organizer below may help students with this preparation.

Task: Compare and contrast Herbert Hoover and Franklin D. Roosevelt's responses to the economic crises of the Great Depression. For additional practice, compare and contrast FDR's response to the Great Depression to Barack Obama's response to the Great Recession.

Text Type	Informative (Compare/contrast)
Text Purpose	Compare/contrast and apply to recent history
Writing Purpose	Compare and contrast how Hoover and Roosevelt responded to the Great Depression. Then compare Obama's response to the recession to FDR's response to the Great Depression.
Signal Words	*Compare:* likewise, similarly, same as, like, similar to, equally *Contrast:* unlike, differ, different from, in contrast, however, on the other hand
Language Usage Goal	*Student chooses a language usage area on which to focus.*

2. Next students need to organize their ideas in a way that fits the conventions of the writing purpose. Since the passage is quite short, a paragraph or two will be sufficient for completing the task. Students should use the same process they used to respond to the *Booker T. Washington and W. E. B. Du Bois*. First have them develop a T-chart as they read through the text. Then, they can populate a Venn with the points on the T-Chart. Finally, have students choose either the Block or the Point-by-Point system to organize the written response.

3. Just like their previous writing practice in the Bridging Reading activity, provide students with a reference list of signal words for compare and contrast (such as the list on page 24 of the Comparisons and Contrasts lesson).

4. Based on the area of language usage students have chosen to target, provide resources to help them revise their writing. At first, this may require the teacher to identify the problem area. However, with consistent exposure to self and peer editing, students should be able to identify such areas in their own and their peers' writing.

5. Provide students access to additional resources about Obama's response to the Great Recession. Guide them in similar bridging activities to analyze and synthesize the resource. Finally, support them in synthesizing the two resources into one compare/contrast essay by following Bridging Written Response strategies 1–4.

➢ Bridging Language Usage

Strategy 1: *Determine and target areas of language usage that require further development.*

Strategy 2: *Analyze specific areas of language usage as modeled in authentic and relevant communication tasks.*

Strategy 3: *Develop specific areas of language usage through participation in authentic communication tasks.*

Strategy 4: *Revise language usage by utilizing peer- and self-editing checklists, rubrics, and language resources.*

1. Determine the language needs of the students and choose a particular language usage area to focus on for this lesson. As an example, let's focus on a review of simple, compound, and complex sentences.

2. Throughout the first three lessons students have had the opportunity to analyze various sentence structures. Using varied sentence structure is an important element in producing quality writing. First, review the elements of simple, compound, and complex sentences. Then, return to the text, and have students find examples of each and dissect them for their component parts. This graphic organizer may help them with this.

Simple Sentences Underline subject once, verb twice	**Compound Sentences** Underline subjects once, verbs twice; circle coordinating conjunction	**Complex Sentences** Underline subjects once, verbs twice; circle signal word
What followed was the worst economic depression in U.S. history.	*By the end of Hoover's presidency, economic recovery had not occurred, and Hoover was very unpopular with the American people.*	*Just months after he was elected president, the stock market crash of 1929 occurred.*

3. As mentioned in Strategy 2, students need to return to a contextualized communicative activity (the whole) to apply their analysis. Using the sentences they found in the text as models, students need to include a variety of sentence structures in their written response activities.

4. To revise problematic areas of usage, students can use peer editing. Students can peer edit for inclusion of sentence variety using the Editing Rubric (p. 131). They should identify the signal word (if present), subject, and verb (with negative) in each sentence and circle any problem areas. Ask them to make suggestions on how to correct these areas. They might continue through the checklist to evaluate other areas of language usage, but do not specifically identify these or offer suggestions. Have students meet, share feedback, and revise their writing. Pay attention to supporting constructive peer conversations (see Discourse Prompts, p. 136).

Hoover did not believe in government assistance for its people; however, this was not the case with FDR.

Although Hoover later, it was too late.

What did he do later?

➢ Assessment & Next Steps

Students should complete the suggested practice activities and the activities included in each lesson. Evaluate which learning goals were not met and remediate by using other resources, such as those identified in the Bridging Knowledge section. Upon successful completion, continue to the next lesson.

CAUSE-AND-EFFECT RELATIONSHIPS

Skills-Based Questions

1. What do cause-and-effect relationships explain?

2. How are cause-and-effect relationships described in the text?

	Learning Goals:	**GED**
Knowledge Goals:	1. Determine cause-and-effect relationships in text.	R.3.3
Reading Goals:	1. Describe cause-and-effect relationships in the text.	R.3.3
	2. Make inferences about relationships between ideas in a text, such as cause-and-effect.	R.3.4
	3. Identify signal words that show cause and effect in the text.	R.5.3
Vocabulary Goals:	1. Define key subject and academic vocabulary.	R.4.1
	2. Determine the meaning of unknown vocabulary using context clues, word forms, and parts of speech.	
	3. Produce writing and speech using new vocabulary.	
Written Response Goals:	1. Use main ideas and text details to show cause-and-effect relationships in writing.	W.1
	2. Respond to text by describing cause-and-effect relationships from the text, organizing the text to support this, and focusing on the writing task.	W.2 W.3
	3. Use standard English language conventions. *(See Language Usage Goals)*	
Language Usage Goals:	1. Identify and correct fragment sentences.	L.2.2
	2. Identify and correct errors in complex subject-verb agreement.	L.1.7
	3. Edit writing to include a variety of sentence structures with appropriate transition words and punctuation.	L.1.9

Sample Instructional Support Strategies

➢ **Bridging Knowledge**

> **Strategy 1:** *Develop prior knowledge and skills to connect to new knowledge.*
>
> **Strategy 2:** *Use guiding questions to make connections beyond the lesson to broader life themes and topics.*
>
> **Strategy 3:** *Use reading strategies to develop, monitor, and synthesize new knowledge. (See Bridging Reading)*
>
> **Strategy 4:** *Demonstrate (and further develop) synthesis of new knowledge through written student response tasks. (See Bridging Written Response)*

1. Evaluate students' knowledge of the following language arts concepts and skills. Utilize the chart below to develop student background knowledge and skills as necessary.

Cause-and-Effect Relationships	Reading Cause and Effect	Writing Cause and Effect	Language Usage Varied Sentence Structure Subject-Verb Agreement
Writing for the GED Test Book 1: Grammar, Usage, and Mechanics			Sentence Fragments (p. 26); Subject-Verb Agreement III (p. 52); Commas (p. 66); Semicolons (p. 68)
Core Skills in Reading & Writing	Unit 3, Lesson 3: Text Structure (p. 62)	Unit 5, Lessons 1: Topic Sentences (p. 115); Lesson 2: Supporting Details (p. 118); Lesson 3: Transitions (p. 121) Unit 6, Lesson 1: Types of Essays (p. 125)	Unit 4, Lesson 2: Sentence Structure (p. 84) Lesson 4: Commas (p. 92) Lesson 6: Agreement (p. 99)
Scoreboost: Writing Across the Tests Sentence Structure, Usage, and Mechanics (SS); Responding to Text (RT)			SS: Correct Sentence Fragments (p. 10); Make Subjects and Verbs Agree in Complicated Sentence Structures (p. 22)
Scoreboost: Thinking Skills Critical Thinking	Interpret Cause and Effect (p. 18)	Interpret Cause and Effect (p. 18)	
Pre-HSE Workbook Reading (R); Writing 1 (W1); Writing 2 (W2)	R: Cause and Effect (p. 24)		W1: Subject-Verb Agreement (p. 30); Sentence Fragments (p. 42)

2. Contextualize the GED Application portion of the lesson (p. 34) within a broader theme or topic by beginning the lesson with Guiding Questions. Guiding questions that are authentic and relevant to students draw them deeper into the lesson and allow them to build deeper knowledge beyond the content of the lesson.

> **Guiding Questions:**
>
> 1. Why do the trees in the redwood forest grow so big and so old? How does this happen?
>
> 2. How are old-growth redwood forests different than new-growth ones and why?

➤ **Bridging Reading**

> **Strategy 1:** Determine the type of text, establish reading purpose, and make predictions using text features and signal words.
>
> **Strategy 2:** Develop text analysis using think-alouds, annotation, sentence frames, and graphic organizers.
>
> **Strategy 3:** Overcome text analysis barriers using prior knowledge, analyzing language usage, and using resources.
>
> **Strategy 4:** Synthesize text analysis using paraphrasing, text frames, graphic organizers, and peer discussions.

1. Have students use pre-reading strategies (p. 8) to scan the text features and signal words to determine the type of text, its purpose, the purpose of the reading task (test prompt or question), and make predictions about the text. Given only a few obvious text features or clues, students may scan the first paragraph. A graphic organizer may be helpful for noting this information.

Example: Guided Practice (p. 32), *Heat Wave*

	Answers	**Text Features**	**Signal Words**
Text Type	Informational	Title	Scientific environmental words, agencies, and measurements
Text Purpose	Informative: cause and effect	Questions in the margins	In questions: causal chain, cause-and-effect relationship In text: trigger, continues, dramatic effect, that would mean
Reading Purpose	Answer questions about cause and effect	The questions in margins	Same as above
Prediction	Will tell how rising temperatures are affecting the Earth	Title, the questions in margins	Same as above

2. The Guided Practice portion of the lesson utilizes annotation strategies and a graphic organizer to model the text analysis process students can use for the GED Application portion. The lesson's featured graphic organizer, however, is to synthesize the complete text, not to aid students in understanding each section of the text. Therefore, identifying smaller cause-and-effect relationships while annotating each section will help students develop this understanding. In addition, modeling this analysis with a think-aloud will help students discover these embedded cause-and-effect relationships.

> **Example:** Think-aloud for Heat Wave, paragraph 2:
>
> The first sentence starts with the subject "One." This refers back to the last line of the previous paragraph that references the "far-reaching effects" of "warmer temperatures." So the "melting of the polar ice caps" is one of the effects of "warmer temperatures." I can note this by showing the cause-and-effect relationship this way: [*warm temps* ➔ *melting of polar ice caps*]. The text describes this further, saying the ice is "rapidly shrinking." "Shrinking" means "getting smaller," which for ice is the same as melting. It goes on to say that if "the trend continues," there will be no ice in the summer by the mid-2000s. This is "raising sea levels," so, I can add this to my causal chain: [*warm temps* ➔ *melting of polar ice caps* ➔ *no ice in summer by mid 2000s* ➔ *raising sea levels*]

3. Like compare and contrast, cause and effect also uses distinct language that can help ELLs recognize this relationship. Although there are a number of signal words that are obvious (see page 30 in the Cause-and-Effect Relationships lesson), there are also a number that are less so. This is because verbs that describe change are often used to show the effect of the subject on the object. These will not always show cause and effect, but once a student has identified that the purpose of a text is to demonstrate this relationship, it will become easier for students to recognize these words. Here are some such examples to share with students:

> ***Verbs that signal change:*** *make, create, increase, decrease, change, trigger, cause, affect, shrink, grow, spread, produce, stimulate, result, improve, worsen*

4. Although there is no oral response required for the GED test, oral text response is an effective way for students to synthesize and develop their understanding of the text. In addition, group discussion allows ELLS to collaborate and build a greater knowledge of the content and of language usage to better prepare for a written or assessment task. Consider having students create oral causal chains in small groups. Give each group a set of note cards. On each note card feature a primary cause from the reading. Student 1 begins the causal chain by stating what is on the card as the cause of (blank). Student 2 must complete the sentence with a signal verb and the first effect in the chain. Then Student 2 starts the next sentence by stating the effect as a cause of (blank) . Student 3 completes that sentence with a signal verb and the next effect and so on until there are no further known effects of the primary cause. Then students begin again with the next card.

Example: Oral causal chain using _Heat Wave_

Card	Student Responses
Burning fossil fuel	Student 1: _Burning fossil fuel causes …_ Student 2: _the polar ice caps to melt. The melting of the polar ice caps triggers …_ Student 3: _rising sea levels. Rising sea levels result in …_ Student 1: _Flooding of coastal areas. Flooding of coastal areas create …_ Student 2: _Property damage and loss of life. Property damage and loss of life affect …_

➢ **Bridging Vocabulary**

> _**Strategy 1:**_ _**Identify the component parts and usage of new words to interpret their meanings.**_
>
> _**Strategy 2:**_ _**Use context clues to interpret new words, including figurative and connotative language.**_
>
> _**Strategy 3:**_ _**Utilize vocabulary-building resources.**_
>
> _**Strategy 4:**_ _**Build a deeper knowledge of words through writing and speaking tasks.**_

1. First, present the shortest form of the word (the base word, often the verb form), followed by other commonly used word forms (if available). Examine prefixes and suffixes and their impact on word meaning and usage.

2. Read the word as used in the context of the text and discuss possible meanings given context clues and word form.

3. Have students find (electronically or in print) the definition or translation of the base form and, if different, the form used in context and note these definitions for future reference and study.

4. Gradually build a deeper knowledge of the word by having students use the word in a sentence frame, guided discussion, and an original sentence (see Appendix D, p. 144).

➤ **Bridging Written Response**

> **Strategy 1:** *Prepare for a response task by identifying its purpose, audience, signal words, structure, and style.*
>
> **Strategy 2:** *Organize text analysis for a written response using a graphic organizer and/or paragraph/essay frame.*
>
> **Strategy 3:** *Overcome barriers to producing clear/coherent writing by using models, language analysis, and resources.*
>
> **Strategy 4:** *Revise writing by utilizing peer- and self-editing checklists, rubrics, and writing resources.*
>
> Strategy 5: *Extend text analysis to build upon initial information or claims by using evidence from additional sources.*

1. To prepare for the response task, students need to identify the writing purpose (based on the writing prompt), the language they will use to meet their purpose (the signal words), and the area of language usage on which they will focus (Language Usage Goals). The graphic organizer below may help students with this preparation.

Task: Summarize how the trees in the redwood forest grow so big and so old. In addition, describe how old trees and new trees have different impacts on the ecology of the forest. Remember to use signal words/verbs.

Text Type	Informative (cause/effect)
Text Purpose	Describe cause and effect within the redwood forest
Writing Purpose	Summarize how old trees create the ecology of the redwood forest. Explain how old and new trees have different effects on the ecology of the forest.
Signal Words	*Cause:* due to, since, in order to, because of, as, so as to, so that, given that *Effect:* therefore, consequently, as a result, then, for this reason, thus *Verbs:* make, create, increase, change, trigger, cause, affect, produce, provide
Language Usage Goal	*Student chooses a language usage area on which to focus.*

2. Given an oral practice such as the example in Bridging Reading, students should be able to move those causal chains from speaking to writing. This time, however, they need to begin with a topic sentence, end with a conclusion, and logically sequence the causal chains in between. If students have a set of cards from the conversation activity related to the *Ecology of the Redwood Forest* reading, they can sequence these first and then transfer their oral chains to written sentences.

Dense fog	Redwoods capture moisture	Redwoods lose foliage	Large plant communities	Young trees
1	2	3	4	5

3. Again, as in the previous writing practice from the Bridging Reading activity, provide students with a reference list of signal words (including verbs) for cause and effect.

4. Based on the area of language usage students have chosen to target, provide resources to help them revise their writing. At first, this may require the teacher to identify the problem area. However, with consistent exposure to self and peer editing, students should be able to identify such areas in their own and their peers' writing.

➤ Bridging Language Usage

> **Strategy 1:** *Determine and target areas of language usage that require further development.*
>
> **Strategy 2:** *Analyze specific areas of language usage as modeled in authentic and relevant communication tasks.*
>
> **Strategy 3:** *Develop specific areas of language usage through participation in authentic communication tasks.*
>
> **Strategy 4:** *Revise language usage by utilizing peer- and self-editing checklists, rubrics, and language resources.*

1. Determine the language needs of the students and choose a particular language usage area to focus on for this lesson. As an example, let's focus on identifying and correcting fragments and subject-verb agreement.

2. Throughout several lessons, students have had the opportunity to analyze various sentence structures and complete subject-verb agreement practices. Now students need to be able to identify fragment sentences and correct them. Furthermore, they will need to use correct subject-verb agreement. The activity in Bridging Reading Strategy 4 provides a great way to integrate this language usage. Prior to beginning the activity, use one causal chain to model how to complete fragment sentences with subject-verb agreement.

Card	Sentence fragment	Complete the fragment with subject-verb agreement
Burning fossil fuel	Burning fossil fuel … The melting of the polar ice caps … Rising sea levels … Flooding of coastal areas … Property damage and loss of life …	**causes** the polar ice caps to melt. **triggers** rising sea levels. **result** in flooding of coastal areas. **causes** property damage and loss of life. _____.

3. As mentioned in Strategy 2, students need to return to a contextualized communicative activity (the whole) to apply their analysis. Continuing from the example above, students can participate in the oral causal chain activity and actively apply this language usage.

4. Students need regular practice composing in a word processing program. As students move on to college or into the workforce, they will need to word process their written responses, from simple emails to complex research papers. The added benefit of these programs is their built-in spelling and grammar checks. Word processing programs readily point out fragment sentences and improper subject-verb agreement using a standard convention like a dotted underline, for example. Point out these identifiers to students and use them to their advantage.

➤ Assessment & Next Steps

Students should complete the suggested practice activities and the activities included in each lesson. Evaluate which learning goals were not met and remediate by using other resources, such as those identified in the Bridging Knowledge section. Upon successful completion, continue to the next lesson.

LANGUAGE: MEANING AND TONE

Skills-Based Questions

1. How does word choice affect the meaning and tone of a text?

2. How can you determine the meaning of unknown words without a dictionary?

	Learning Goals:	**GED**
Knowledge Goals:	1. Determine how word choice affects the meaning and tone of a text.	R.4.2
	2. Use context clues to guess the meaning of unknown words.	R.4.1
Reading Goals:	1. Determine meaning (including connotations) of unknown words from context clues.	R.4.1
	2. Describe the tone of a text and identify words and phrases that support that tone.	R.4.2
	3. Determine the author's purpose for word choice.	R.4.3
Vocabulary Goals:	1. Define key subject and academic vocabulary.	R.4.1
	2. Determine the meaning of unknown vocabulary using context clues, word forms, and parts of speech.	
	3. Produce writing and speech using new vocabulary.	
Written Response Goals:	1. Make an argument and support it with details from the text.	W.1
	2. Respond to text by describing the effect of word choice on meaning and tone, organizing the text to support this, and focusing on the writing task.	W.2
		W.3
	3. Use standard English language conventions. *(See Language Usage Goals)*	
Language Usage Goals:	1. Identify and correct run-on sentences and comma splices with correct punctuation.	L.2.2
	2. Edit writing to include a variety of sentence structures with appropriate transition words and punctuation.	L.2.4
		L.1.9

Sample Instructional Support Strategies

➢ Bridging Knowledge

Strategy 1: *Develop prior knowledge and skills to connect to new knowledge.*

Strategy 2: *Use guiding questions to make connections beyond the lesson to broader life themes and topics.*

Strategy 3: *Use reading strategies to develop, monitor, and synthesize new knowledge.* (See Bridging Reading)

Strategy 4: *Demonstrate (and further develop) synthesis of new knowledge through written student response tasks.* (See Bridging Written Response)

1. Evaluate students' knowledge of the following language arts concepts and skills. Utilize the chart below to develop student background knowledge and skills as necessary.

Language: Meaning and Tone	Reading Meaning and Tone	Writing Meaning and Tone	Language Usage Run-ons; Comma splices
Writing for the GED Test Book 1: Grammar, Usage, and Mechanics			Run-ons and Comma Splices (p. 28) Commas (p. 66) Semicolons (p. 68)
Core Skills in Reading & Writing	Unit 1, Lesson 5: Mood and Tone (p. 25) Unit 3, Lesson 7: Understanding Vocabulary (p. 73)	Unit 5, Lesson 1: Topic Sentences (p. 115); Lesson 2: Supporting Details (p. 118); Lesson 3: Transitions (p. 121)	Unit 4, Lesson 2: Sentence Structure (p. 84); Lesson 4: Commas (p. 92)
Scoreboost: Writing Across the Tests Sentence Structure, Usage, and Mechanics (SS); Responding to Text (RT)		RT: Use Varied and Precise Words (p. 19)	SS: Correct Run-Ons and Fused Sentences (p. 4); Use Commas Correctly (p. 32)
Scoreboost: Thinking Skills Critical Thinking			
Pre-HSE Workbook Reading (R); Writing 1 (W1); Writing 2 (W2)	R: Tone (p. 30)		W1: Run-ons and Comma Splices (p. 40)

2. Contextualize the GED Application portion of the lesson (p. 40) within a broader theme or topic by beginning the lesson with Guiding Questions. Guiding questions that are authentic and relevant to students draw them deeper into the lesson and allow them to build deeper knowledge beyond the content of the lesson.

Guiding Questions:

1. How does the author's word choice and tone in the excerpt from *The Story of an Eyewitness* emphasize the power of nature?

2. How does this event, as it is described, improve our understanding of the relationship between human beings and nature?

➢ **Bridging Reading**

> **Strategy 1:** Determine the type of text, establish reading purpose, and make predictions using text features and signal words.
>
> **Strategy 2:** Develop text analysis using think-alouds, annotation, sentence frames, and graphic organizers.
>
> **Strategy 3:** Overcome text analysis barriers using prior knowledge, analyzing language usage, and using resources.
>
> **Strategy 4:** Synthesize text analysis using paraphrasing, text frames, graphic organizers, and peer discussions.

1. Have students use pre-reading strategies (p. 8) to scan the text features and signal words to determine the type of text, its purpose, the purpose of the reading task (test prompt or question), and to make predictions about the text. Given only a few obvious text features or clues, students may scan the first paragraph. A graphic organizer may be helpful for noting this information.

Example: Guided Practice (p. 38), excerpt from *Life on the Mississippi*

	Answers	Text Features	Signal Words
Text Type	Narrative	Title	"Life" "When I was a boy…"
Text Purpose	To tell a true story	Title, beginning phrase of each paragraph	"When I was a boy," "After all these years"
Reading Purpose	Answer questions about vocabulary and tone	the directions, the questions in margins	"What does transient mean?" "What words describe"
Prediction	Will tell about his life on the Mississippi	Title, beginning phrase of each paragraph	Same as above

2. The Guided Practice portion of the lesson utilizes annotation strategies and a graphic organizer to model the text analysis process students can use for the GED Application portion. However, additional annotations (p. 9) are helpful to note overall main idea of passage; identify confusing words or passages of the text as they note who, where, when, what's happening, and why/how (if applicable) for each paragraph; and return to confusing areas of the text and interpret words and dissect confusing, complex sentences. For the third read-through, have students focus on understanding confusing areas of text based on the context before they consult a resource. For example, students can read the text around the confusing words and phrases, and underline any context clues. In pairs, have students "think-aloud" to discuss their guesses and support them with the context clues they found.

> **Example:** Guided Practice think-aloud:
>
> *"I didn't understand the word '**tilted**' in paragraph 2. The text says '…one or two clerks sitting in front of the Water Street stores, with their splint-bottomed chairs **tilted** back against the wall, chins on breasts, hats slouched over their faces, asleep…' I think '**tilted**' means going back with your body like this [student leans back], because the text says 'tilted **back against the wall**' like this [student leans back again]. Another context clue is that they are '**asleep**' and have their '**chins on breasts**.' That makes me think they are really comfortable and relaxing back."*

3. Generally, language acquisition researchers say that you need to understand between 95% and 98% of the surrounding text to "guess" vocabulary in context. ELLs will most likely not have this level of understanding and will need additional tools. A five-step process is helpful (see the flowchart below).

   1. Read the sentence for gist: who, where, when, what (are they doing/is happening/is the problem/ etc.).

   2. Read the text (phrases or clauses) around the word and use context clues.

   3. Determine the part of speech of the unknown word.

   4. Study the word's base/prefix/suffix.

5. In a testing situation, try each possible answer from the test question and choose the one that sounds the best. Not testing? Consult a dictionary or translator.

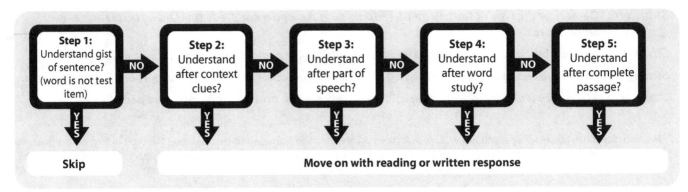

4. For the Guided Practice portion of this lesson, consider this guiding question:

> How does the author's word choice and tone in the excerpt from *Life on the Mississippi* emphasize his boyhood ambition to be a steamboatman?

The skills introduction of this lesson (p. 36) provides a graphic organizer that illustrates word connotation. Have students choose 10 words from paragraph 2 that show the author's "positive" connotation of steamboats and put them in the chart. Then have them fill out "neutral" and "negative" words of similar denotative meaning for each of the 10 words. This is a great time to use a thesaurus. Finally, have them write a description of the steamboat using either the neutral or negative words instead of the positive ones (see example below). Discuss how this word choice affects the tone of the piece.

Positive Connotations (from excerpt)	Neutral Connotation	Negative Connotation
1. sharp and trim	angled and fit	edgy and bony
2. fancy-topped	formally-topped	garishly-topped
3. ornamented	decorated	overloaded
Example: *The steamboat was edgy and bony, with two garishly-topped chimneys and its deck overloaded with white railings.*		

➤ Bridging Vocabulary

> **Strategy 1:** *Identify the component parts and usage of new words to interpret their meanings.*
>
> **Strategy 2:** *Use context clues to interpret new words, including figurative and connotative language.*
>
> **Strategy 3:** *Utilize vocabulary-building resources.*
>
> **Strategy 4:** *Build a deeper knowledge of words through writing and speaking tasks.*

1. First, present the shortest form of the word (the base word, often the verb form), followed by other commonly used word forms (if available). Examine prefixes and suffixes and their impact on word meaning and usage.

2. Read the word as used in the context of the text and discuss possible meanings given context clues and word form.

3. Have students find (electronically or in print) the definition or translation of the base form and, if different, the form used in context and note these definitions for future reference and study.

4. Gradually build a deeper knowledge of the word by having students use the word in a sentence frame, guided discussion, and an original sentence (see Appendix D, p. 144).

➤ **Bridging Written Response**

> **Strategy 1:** *Prepare for a response task by identifying its purpose, audience, signal words, structure, and style.*
>
> **Strategy 2:** *Organize text analysis for a written response using a graphic organizer and/or paragraph/essay frame.*
>
> **Strategy 3:** *Overcome barriers to producing clear/coherent writing by using models, language analysis, and resources.*
>
> **Strategy 4:** *Revise writing by utilizing peer- and self-editing checklists, rubrics, and writing resources.*
>
> **Strategy 5:** *Extend text analysis to build upon initial information or claims by using evidence from additional sources.*

1. To prepare for the response task, students need to identify the writing purpose (based on the writing prompt), the language they will use to meet their purpose (the signal words), and the area of language usage on which they will focus (Language Usage Goals). The graphic organizer below may help students with this preparation.

Task: Write a paragraph describing how the author's word choice and tone in the excerpt from *The Story of an Eyewitness* emphasizes the power of nature. Include a topic sentence that states your argument, three details to support it, and a concluding sentence. Make sure to describe each example's connotation and effect on tone.

Text Type	Argument
Text Purpose	Describe the author's use of word choice and tone to support an argument.
Writing Purpose	Write an argument that states how the author's word choice and tone emphasize the power of nature. Include examples with connotation and tone.
Signal Words	*Cause (word choice):* due to, since, because of, as, so as to, so that, given that *Effect (tone):* therefore, consequently, as a result, then, for this reason, thus *Examples:* for example, such as, including, one example is, for instance, to illustrate
Language Usage Goal	*Student chooses a language usage area on which to focus.*

2. Students can use a graphic organizer to set up their written response.

Topic Sentence: *(state your argument)*			
	Word Choice	**Connotation**	**Tone**
Example 1:	*smoke = lurid tower*	*ominous, scary*	*fear*
Example 2:	*smashed by the earthquake*	*powerful, dangerous,*	*devastation*
Example 3:	*fled*	*devastated, victims*	*despair*
Concluding Sentence: *(state the conclusion of your argument)*			

3. As students become familiar with presenting arguments, they will learn how to effectively use text evidence to support their arguments. Using signal words that introduce text evidence help students learn to do this.

> ***According to*** the text/author _____.
>
> The text/author **says** _____.
>
> In paragraph 2, the text **states** _____.
>
> The author **uses** the word/phrase _____ to _____.
>
> One line in the text **that shows this** is _____.

4. Based on the area of language usage students have chosen to target, provide resources to help them revise their writing. At first, this may require the teacher to identify the problem area. However, with consistent exposure to self and peer editing, students should be able to identify such areas in their own and their peers' writing.

5. Although this example does not use resources to extend content knowledge, it is an example of using resources to extend language knowledge. Using a graphic organizer similar to the one in Bridging Reading Strategy 4, have students choose 10 emotional words from the *Story of an Eyewitness* excerpt. Then, have them consult a thesaurus and write down a neutral connotation for each word they chose. Finally, they will rewrite the narrative as a newspaper report, using a neutral tone.

Emotional	smashed	humped	shrewd contrivances	thrown out of gear
Neutral	brought down	filled	equipment	ruined

Example: *The earthquake brought down the buildings, filled the streets with debris, and ruined the city's equipment and safeguards.*

➤ Bridging Language Usage

Strategy 1: *Determine and target areas of language usage that require further development.*

Strategy 2: *Analyze specific areas of language usage as modeled in authentic and relevant communication tasks.*

Strategy 3: *Develop specific areas of language usage through participation in authentic communication tasks.*

Strategy 4: Revise language usage by utilizing peer- and self-editing checklists, rubrics and language resources.

1. Determine the language needs of the students and choose a particular language usage area to focus on for this lesson. As an example, let's focus on identifying and correcting run-on sentences and comma splices.

2. Paragraph 2 of the Guided Practice presents an excellent example of long, compound, complex sentences. Rewrite the paragraph without punctuation and project it for students to read aloud. This will give them a sense of why punctuation is important for comprehension. Cut a copy of this rewritten paragraph into sections and have students, in pairs, add punctuation to their section. Then have each student pair seek out other pairs to reconstruct the complete paragraph. Together, the larger group will check over the complete paragraph and then check it against the original.

3. Reinforce the accurate construction of sentences and elimination of run-ons and comma splices during the Bridging Written Response task for Strategies 3 and 5.

➤ Assessment & Next Steps

Students should complete the suggested practice activities and the activities included in each lesson. Evaluate which learning goals were not met and remediate by using other resources, such as those identified in the Bridging Knowledge section. Upon successful completion, continue to the Cumulative Review and then onto the Reading Fiction lessons.

Reading Fiction

PLOT

Skills-Based Questions

1. What parts of a story make up its plot?
2. How does each part of the plot lead to the next?

	Learning Goals:	GED
Knowledge Goals:	1. Describe the parts of a plot and how they lead from one to the other.	R.3.3
		R.5.2
Reading Goals:	1. Make inferences about plot, characters, settings, or ideas in text.	R.3.2
	2. Describe how events in a text contribute to the plot or conflict.	R.3.3
	3. Describe how parts of the text (words, phrases, clauses, and paragraphs) relate to other parts of the text.	R.5.2
Vocabulary Goals:	1. Define key subject and academic vocabulary.	R.4.1
	2. Determine the meaning of unknown vocabulary using context clues, word forms, and parts of speech.	
	3. Produce writing and speech using new vocabulary.	
Written Response Goals:	1. Describe how the text demonstrates the parts of a plot and support this with details from the text.	W.1
		W.2
	2. Respond to text by describing how the parts of the plot work together to tell a story, organizing the text to support this, and focusing on the writing task.	W.3
	3. Use standard English language conventions. *(See Language Usage Goals)*	
Language Usage Goals:	1. Identify and correct fragments, run-on sentences and comma splices with correct punctuation.	L.2.2
		L.2.4
	2. Edit writing to include a variety of sentence structures with appropriate transition words and punctuation.	L.1.9

Sample Instructional Support Strategies

➢ Bridging Knowledge

> **Strategy 1:** *Develop prior knowledge and skills to connect to new knowledge.*
>
> **Strategy 2:** *Use guiding questions to make connections beyond the lesson to broader life themes and topics.*
>
> **Strategy 3:** *Use reading strategies to develop, monitor, and synthesize new knowledge.* (See Bridging Reading)
>
> **Strategy 4:** *Demonstrate (and further develop) synthesis of new knowledge through written student response tasks.* (See Bridging Written Response)

1. Evaluate students' knowledge of the following language arts concepts and skills. Utilize the chart below to develop student background knowledge and skills as necessary.

	Plot	Reading	Writing	Language Usage
		Plot	Plot	Run-ons and Comma Splices
Writing for the GED Test Book 1: Grammar, Usage, and Mechanics				Sentence Fragments (p. 26); Run-ons and Comma Splices (p. 28); Other Kinds of Pronouns (p. 40); Commas (p. 66); Semicolons (p. 68)
Core Skills in Reading & Writing	Unit 1, Lesson 4: Plot (p. 21)		Unit 5, Lesson 1: Topic Sentences (p. 115); Lesson 2: Supporting Details (p. 118); Lesson 3: Transitions (p. 121)	Unit 4, Lesson 2: Sentence Structure (p. 84); Lesson 4: Commas (p. 92)
Scoreboost: Writing Across the Tests Sentence Structure, Usage, and Mechanics (SS); Responding to Text (RT)			RT: Use Varied and Precise Words (p. 19)	SS: Correct Run-Ons and Fused Sentences (p. 4); Correct Sentence Fragments (p. 10); Use Commas Correctly (p. 32)
Pre-HSE Workbook Reading (R); Writing 1 (W1); Writing 2 (W2)	R: Plot and Conflict (p. 44)			W1: Run-Ons and Comma Splices (p. 40); Sentence Fragments (p. 42)

2. Contextualize the GED Application portion of the lesson (p. 50) within a broader theme or topic by beginning the lesson with Guiding Questions. Guiding questions that are authentic and relevant to students draw them deeper into the lesson and allow them to build deeper knowledge beyond the content of the lesson.

> **Guiding Questions:**
>
> 1. How does each component of the plot of *Legend of the Buffalo* demonstrate the values of the Blackfoot?
>
> 2. What does the resolution of the central conflict of the story tell us about the Blackfoot and their relationship with the buffalo?

➢ Bridging Reading

> **Strategy 1:** *Determine the type of text, establish reading purpose, and make predictions using text features and signal words.*
>
> **Strategy 2:** *Develop text analysis using think-alouds, annotation, sentence frames, and graphic organizers.*
>
> **Strategy 3:** *Overcome text analysis barriers using prior knowledge, analyzing language usage, and using resources.*
>
> **Strategy 4:** *Synthesize text analysis using paraphrasing, text frames, graphic organizers, and peer discussions.*

1. Have students use pre-reading strategies (p. 8) to scan the text features and signal words to determine the type of text, its purpose, the purpose of the reading task (test prompt or question), and make predictions about the text. Given only a few obvious text features or clues, students may scan the first paragraph. A graphic organizer may be helpful for noting this information.

Example: Guided Practice (p. 48), *Cherokee Myth of the Pleiades*

	Answers	**Text Features**	**Signal Words**
Text Type	Myth	Title	"Myth,""When the earth was new…"
Text Purpose	To tell a story that explains how something came to be	Title	Same as above
Reading Purpose	Answer questions about conflict and plot	The directions, the questions in margins	"What conflict,""What actions," "story's plot"
Prediction	Will tell how the Pleiades came to be: the boys do something and the mothers are angry	Title, beginning phrase of each paragraph	"seven Cherokee boys," "the mothers became fed up,""the boys rushed off"

2. Annotation strategies (p. 9) help students make meaning from fictional text as well as nonfictional text. However, students need to look for different text elements to help shape that meaning. Here is a sample annotation for three readings of the *Cherokee Myth of the Pleiades*. The first read identifies characters, setting, central conflict, and resolution by answering *who, where, when,* and *what*. On the second read through, students identify confusing words or passages to help build greater understanding of the details of the text as they note *who, where, when, what's happening,* and *why* for each paragraph. Finally, students return to confusing areas of the text and interpret words using vocabulary strategies and dissect confusing, complex sentences for subject, verb, phrases, and dependent clauses.

Example: Guided Practice, Annotation

1. **Who:** *Cherokee boys and mothers*
   Where: *in their town*
   When: *when the earth was young*
   What: *The boys are playing too much and not helping their families and the mothers are angry*
   What: *The boys become the constellation the Pleiades; one became the pine tree*

2. *"absorbed in their play" (didn't pay attention to chores); "mothers scolded them" (yelled at them)*

3. *Paragraph 2:*
   Who: *the mothers and boys*
   Where: *at home for dinner*
   When: *dinnertime*
   What's happening: *mothers put stones in corn*
   Why: *because boys wouldn't listen to their mothers.*

3. Student peers are powerful resources in the classroom. When students are struggling with text analysis, pairing them with a partner can provide the support they need. This could be a partner of equal or greater skill in the area of text analysis. Equal-ability pairing holds each learner accountable, as neither has the expertise required to master the task alone. Through negotiation, equal-ability pairs may arrive at the desired outcome or approximations of it. With unequal-ability pairing, the higher-ability partner coaches the struggling partner toward the desired outcome. Without this "coaching" element, the effectiveness of unequal-ability pairing is questionable, and could enable the struggling partner instead of support. Here is some collaborative language that may be helpful in facilitating either pairing. Provide students with some discourse prompts (Appendix B, p. 136) to encourage discussion.

Disagree politely: *I see what you're saying but _____. Another way to think about this is _____. Have you thought about _____?*

Encourage participation: *I'd like to hear what you have to say about _____. Do you have anything more to add?*

Probe others' contributions: *Could you explain that further? What did you mean by _____? Can you give me an example?*

4. The Guided Practice portion of this lesson provides a graphic organizer for students to synthesize their understanding of the story's plot by entering the events of the story into their corresponding plot component boxes. A variation on this would be to have students write a summary sentence for each paragraph using their annotations and then add their sentences into the provided graphic organizer.

> **Example: Paragraph 2 [Rising Action]:**
> *The mothers put stones in the boys' corn at dinnertime because they were angry at the boys for not listening to them.*

➢ Bridging Vocabulary

> **Strategy 1:** *Identify the component parts and usage of new words to interpret their meanings.*
>
> **Strategy 2:** *Use context clues to interpret new words, including figurative and connotative language.*
>
> **Strategy 3:** *Utilize vocabulary-building resources.*
>
> **Strategy 4:** *Build a deeper knowledge of words through writing and speaking tasks.*

1. First, present the shortest form of the word (the base word, often the verb form), followed by other commonly used word forms (if available). Examine prefixes and suffixes and their impact on word meaning and usage.

2. Read the word as used in the context of the text and discuss possible meanings given context clues and word form.

3. Have students find (electronically or in print) the definition or translation of the base form and, if different, the form used in context and note these definitions for future reference and study.

4. Gradually build a deeper knowledge of the word by having students use the word in a sentence frame, guided discussion, and an original sentence (see Appendix D, p. 144).

➢ Bridging Written Response

> **Strategy 1:** *Prepare for a response task by identifying its purpose, audience, signal words, structure, and style.*
>
> **Strategy 2:** *Organize text analysis for a written response using a graphic organizer and/or paragraph/essay frame.*
>
> Strategy 3: *Overcome barriers to producing clear/coherent writing by using models, language analysis, and resources.*
>
> **Strategy 4:** *Revise writing by utilizing peer- and self-editing checklists, rubrics, and writing resources.*
>
> **Strategy 5:** *Extend text analysis to build upon initial information or claims by using evidence from additional sources.*

1. To prepare for the response task, students need to identify the writing purpose (based on the writing prompt), the language they will use to meet their purpose (the signal words), and the area of language usage on which they will focus (Language Usage Goals). The graphic organizer below may help students with this preparation.

> **Task:** Write a paragraph describing how the events of the story *Legend of the Buffalo* demonstrate the different parts of the plot. Make sure to define each part of the plot and describe an event from the story that demonstrates each part.

Text Type	Informational
Text Purpose	Describe how the story demonstrates the parts of a plot.
Writing Purpose	Write a paragraph to describe how the story shows each part of the plot. Support it with examples from the text.
Signal Words	*Definition:* is defined as, means, is called, referred to as, is when
	Examples: for example, such as, including, one example is, for instance, to illustrate
	Demonstrate: shows, illustrates, represents, reflects
Language Usage Goal	*Student chooses a language usage area on which to focus.*

2. Students can use a paragraph frame to develop their response to the task above.

> ___(The name of the story)___ demonstrates the five parts _____. The first part is the _____. This is defined
> as ___(definition)___. An example from the text is when ___(summary of event)___. _____ is the second part of the plot,
> and this means ___(definition)___. An event in the text that illustrates this is ___(summary of event)___. Next is the _____,
> which means ___(definition)___. One example from the text is ___(summary of event)___. Then comes the _____ defined
> as ___(definition)___. ___(Summary of event)___ is an example of _____. Finally, the _____ ___(definition)___. This
> is demonstrated in the text when ___(summary of event)___.

4. Based on the area of language usage students have chosen to target, provide resources to help them revise their writing. At first, this may require the teacher to identify the problem area. However, with consistent exposure to self and peer editing, students should be able to identify such areas in their own and their peers' writing.

5. The *Legend of the Buffalo* provides insight into Blackfoot cultural values. Have students write a paragraph answering one of the Guiding Questions from Bridging Knowledge. Provide additional resources for students to read in preparation for this task that will help them better understand the events of the story and how they reflect cultural values.

➢ Bridging Language Usage

> **Strategy 1:** *Determine and target areas of language usage that require further development.*
>
> **Strategy 2:** *Analyze specific areas of language usage as modeled in authentic and relevant communication tasks.*
>
> **Strategy 3:** *Develop specific areas of language usage through participation in authentic communication tasks.*
>
> **Strategy 4:** *Revise language usage by utilizing peer- and self-editing checklists, rubrics, and language resources.*

1. Determine the language needs of the students and choose a particular language usage area to focus on for this lesson. As an example, let's focus on identifying and correcting sentence fragments, run-on sentences, and comma splices.

2. Paragraph 3 of the Guided Practice presents an example of long, compound, complex sentences. Rewrite the paragraph without punctuation and project it for students to read aloud. This will give them a sense of why punctuation is important for comprehension. Cut a copy of this rewritten paragraph into sections and have students, in pairs, add punctuation to their section. Then have each student pair seek out other pairs to reconstruct the complete paragraph. Together, the larger group will check over the complete paragraph and then check it against the original.

3. Reinforce the accurate construction of sentences and the elimination of sentence fragments, run-on sentences, and comma splices during the Bridging Written Response task for Strategies 2 and 5.

4. To revise problematic areas of usage, students can use peer editing. Here is an example of how this may look in this lesson given a language usage goal of identifying and eliminating sentence fragments, run-on sentences, and comma splices.

> During the written response task, students can peer edit for sentence fragments, run-on sentences, and comma splices using the Editing Rubric (p. 131). They should identify the subject, predicate, and coordinating conjunction (if any) in each sentence and circle problem areas. Ask them to make suggestions on how to correct these areas. They might continue through the checklist to evaluate other areas of language usage as well, but do not specifically identify these or offer suggestions. Have students meet, share feedback, and revise their writing. Pay attention to supporting constructive peer conversations (see Discourse Prompts, p. 136).

➢ Assessment & Next Steps

Students should complete the suggested practice activities and the activities included in each lesson. Evaluate which learning goals were not met and remediate by using other resources, such as those identified in the Bridging Knowledge section. Upon successful completion, continue to the next lesson.

CHARACTER

Skills-Based Questions

1. How does an author help us get to know a character in a story?
2. How do we use clues to draw conclusions about a character's personality and motivations?

	Learning Goals:	GED
Knowledge Goals:	1. Draw conclusions about a character's appearance, personality, and motivations.	R.3.3
Reading Goals:	1. Make inferences about plot, characters, settings, or ideas in text.	R.3.2
	2. Describe how characters develop in a text.	R.3.3
Vocabulary Goals:	1. Define key subject and academic vocabulary.	R.4.1
	2. Determine the meaning of unknown vocabulary using context clues, word forms, and parts of speech.	
	3. Produce writing and speech using new vocabulary.	
Written Response Goals:	1. Describe a character's appearance, personality, and motivations supported with details from the text.	W.1
		W.2
	2. Respond to text by describing a character's development, organizing the text to support this, and focusing on the writing task.	W.3
	3. Use standard English language conventions. *(See Language Usage Goals)*	
Language Usage Goals:	1. Identify and correct errors in parallelism and coordination.	L.1.6
	2. Use plurals and possessives correctly in writing.	L.1.3
	3. Edit writing to include correct parallelism and coordination.	L.2.3

Sample Instructional Support Strategies

➤ **Bridging Knowledge**

Strategy 1: *Develop prior knowledge and skills to connect to new knowledge.*

Strategy 2: *Use guiding questions to make connections beyond the lesson to broader life themes and topics.*

Strategy 3: *Use reading strategies to develop, monitor, and synthesize new knowledge.* (See Bridging Reading)

Strategy 4: *Demonstrate (and further develop) synthesis of new knowledge through written student response tasks.*
(See Bridging Written Response)

1. Evaluate students' knowledge of the following language arts concepts and skills. Utilize the chart below to develop student background knowledge and skills as necessary.

Character	Reading Character	Writing Character	Language Usage Parallelism and Coordination
Writing for the GED Test Book 1: Grammar, Usage, and Mechanics			Parallelism and Coordination (p. 30); Pronoun-Antecedent Agreement (p. 54); Clear Antecedents (p. 56)
Core Skills in Reading & Writing	Unit 1, Lesson 3: Characterization (p. 18)	Unit 5, Lesson 1: Topic Sentences (p. 115); Lesson 2: Supporting Details (p. 118); Lesson 3: Transitions (p. 121)	
Scoreboost: Writing Across the Tests Sentence Structure, Usage, and Mechanics (SS); Responding to Text (RT)			SS: Coordinate Ideas in Sentences (p. 6); Make Ideas Parallel (p. 14)
Pre-HSE Workbook Reading (R); Writing 1 (W1); Writing 2 (W2)	R: Character (p. 42)		W1: Parallel Form (p. 44); Possessives (p. 20)

2. Contextualize the GED Application portion of the lesson (p. 56) within a broader theme or topic by beginning the lesson with Guiding Questions. Guiding questions that are authentic and relevant to students draw them deeper into the lesson and allow them to build deeper knowledge beyond the content of the lesson.

Guiding Questions:

1. What kinds of character clues about Thomas Gradgrind are presented in the excerpt from *Hard Times*?

2. What do these character clues suggest about Thomas Gradgrind's personality and motivations?

➤ **Bridging Reading**

Strategy 1: *Determine the type of text, establish reading purpose, and make predictions using text features and signal words.*

Strategy 2: *Develop text analysis using think-alouds, annotation, sentence frames, and graphic organizers.*

Strategy 3: *Overcome text analysis barriers using prior knowledge, analyzing language usage, and using resources.*

Strategy 4: *Synthesize text analysis using paraphrasing, text frames, graphic organizers, and peer discussions.*

1. Have students use pre-reading strategies (p. 8) to scan the text features and signal words to determine the type of text, its purpose, the purpose of the reading task (test prompt or question), and to make predictions about the text. Given only a few obvious text features or clues, students may scan the first paragraph. A graphic organizer may be helpful for noting this information.

Example: Guided Practice (p. 54), excerpt from *The Mouse*

	Answers	Text Features	Signal Words
Text Type	Short story excerpt	Title, dialogue	excerpt
Text Purpose	To tell a story about a mouse	Title, dialogue	mouse
Reading Purpose	Answer questions about the character Theodoric	the directions, the questions in margins	key details, Theodoric
Prediction	Theodoric has a problem with a mouse and tells the woman.	Title, questions in margins	"The Mouse," "tell the woman about the mouse"

2. The lesson's introduction (p. 52) provides a chart with the kinds of character clues to look for when determining the appearance and personality of a character. The Guided Practice provides a graphic organizer to match examples from the text to personality traits of the character. A combination of the two graphic organizers, will allow students to really explore the categories of character clues, text examples that represent these categories, and conclusions drawn about a character's personality. In small groups, have each student look for a text example of one of the character clue categories. They can then pool their information.

Character: Theodoric Voler	Author's Description	Character's Appearance	Character's Thoughts	Character's Words	Character's Actions
Text Example	"screened from… the coarser realities of life…"	"scarlet in the face"	"Theodoric accounted abominable …"	"It was a most awkward situation"	"secured the ends of his railway rug"
Conclusion about Personality	shy, proper	embarrassed	proper	embarrassed	modest

3. Fictional texts use an abundance of complex descriptive language that is very challenging for ELLs. Although it is not necessary (nor probable) for them to understand all descriptive language, fictional texts provide an opportunity for them to expand their vocabularies with useful adjectives and descriptive verbs. Prepare a reference sheet of basic character traits and actions to help them with character analysis. Have students use a thesaurus to write down two or three synonyms for each. Have them note in parenthesis the connotation of the trait and each synonym.

Basic Word	Synonym	Synonym
shy (neutral)	timid (more scared)	mousy (negative—wimpy)
remove (neutral)	shed (slip off like a snake)	extricate (get out of/more dangerous)

4. Continuing with the group work from Strategy 2, have students use the information they contributed to the chart to construct a sentence that states their conclusion about the character's personality and support it with an example from the text. Then students can combine their sentences to create a paragraph describing the character.

Example:

Theodoric is a very proper young man because in the text he hangs up a curtain before he takes off his clothes to get the mouse out.

➤ Bridging Vocabulary

> **Strategy 1:** *Identify the component parts and usage of new words to interpret their meanings.*
>
> **Strategy 2:** *Use context clues to interpret new words, including figurative and connotative language.*
>
> **Strategy 3:** *Utilize vocabulary-building resources.*
>
> **Strategy 4:** *Build a deeper knowledge of words through writing and speaking tasks.*

1. First, present the shortest form of the word (the base word, often the verb form), followed by other commonly used word forms (if available). Examine prefixes and suffixes and their impact on word meaning and usage.

2. Read the word as used in the context of the text and discuss possible meanings given context clues and word form.

3. Have students find (electronically or in print) the definition or translation of the base form and, if different, the form used in context and note these definitions for future reference and study.

4. Gradually build a deeper knowledge of the word by having students use the word in a sentence frame, guided discussion, and an original sentence (see Appendix D, p. 144).

➤ Bridging Written Response

> **Strategy 1:** *Prepare for a response task by identifying its purpose, audience, signal words, structure, and style.*
>
> **Strategy 2:** *Organize text analysis for a written response using a graphic organizer and/or paragraph/essay frame.*
>
> **Strategy 3:** *Overcome barriers to producing clear/coherent writing by using models, language analysis, and resources.*
>
> **Strategy 4:** *Revise writing by utilizing peer- and self-editing checklists, rubrics, and writing resources.*
>
> Strategy 5: *Extend text analysis to build upon initial information or claims by using evidence from additional sources.*

1. To prepare for the response task, students need to identify the writing purpose (based on the writing prompt), the language they will use to meet their purpose (the signal words), and the area of language usage on which they will focus (Language Usage Goals). The graphic organizer below may help students with this preparation.

Task: Write a paragraph describing what the different character clues in the excerpt from *Hard Times* suggest about Thomas Gradgrind's personality. Support your conclusions with examples from the text.

Text Type	Fiction
Text Purpose	Make conclusions about the personality and motivations of Thomas Gradgrind
Writing Purpose	Write a paragraph sharing conclusions about the personality and motivations of Thomas Gradgrind. Include examples from the text for support.
Signal Words	*Conclusion:* therefore, thus, in conclusion, as such, given, for this reason *Examples:* for example, such as, including, one example is, for instance, to illustrate *Demonstrate:* shows, illustrates, represents, reflects, demonstrates
Language Usage Goal	*Student chooses a language usage area on which to focus.*

2. Students can use a paragraph frame to develop their response to the task above.

___(Name of character)___ is ___(adjectives to describe his personality)___ . For instance, ___(name of the author)___ illustrates this by describing ___(name of the character)___ as ___(example from text)___ . ___(Name of the character)___ demonstrates that he is ___(adjective)___ when he says ___(quote from text)___ . He also shows his ___(adjective)___ personality when he ___(example from text)___ . Given these examples, ___(name of character)___ is clearly ___(adjectives to describe his personality)___ .

3. In Bridging Reading, students, in small groups, completed a paragraph describing the character Theodoric by combining the sentences they individually wrote. However, most likely these student-generated paragraphs lack the signal words provided in the above paragraph frame. Have students use the paragraph they wrote about Thomas Gadgrind as a model to rewrite their paragraphs about Theodoric.

4. A simple rubric can help students prepare for, compose, and revise their writing. Students can develop the rubric with your help based on the task directions. For example, given the task above, students are required to do three things: 1) Write a paragraph; 2) make conclusions about Thomas Gradgrind's personality; 3) support conclusions with examples from different categories of character clues. A rubric should also describe three or more levels of competency. Decide with your students how to label these levels. Here is an example of a rubric you may develop:

Low	Developing	Sufficient	Strong
Does not state a conclusion.	States an unclear or unsupported conclusion.	States a somewhat supported conclusion about Gradgrind's personality.	States a well-supported conclusion about Gradgrind's personality.
Does not provide appropriate examples.	Provides examples that demonstrate one category of character clues.	Provides supporting examples that demonstrate two or more categories of character clues.	Provides supporting examples that demonstrate three or more categories of character clues.
Does not use any elements of correct paragraph structure.	Uses one element of correct paragraph structure.	Uses two elements of correct paragraph structure.	Uses correct paragraph structure: Topic sentence, supporting details, and concluding sentence.

➤ Bridging Language Usage

> **Strategy 1:** *Determine and target areas of language usage that require further development.*
>
> **Strategy 2:** *Analyze specific areas of language usage as modeled in authentic and relevant communication tasks.*
>
> **Strategy 3:** *Develop specific areas of language usage through participation in authentic communication tasks.*
>
> **Strategy 4:** *Revise language usage by utilizing peer- and self-editing checklists, rubrics, and language resources.*

1. Determine the language needs of the students and choose a particular language usage area to focus on for this lesson. As an example, let's focus on parallelism. (Other choices suggested for this lesson are coordination and pronoun-antecedent agreement and clarity.)

2. From the reading (the context/the whole), choose an example to model the language area of focus (the parts). Here is an example of parallelism from the excerpt from *Hard Times*.

the girl	was	so dark-eyed and dark-haired	that	she		seemed to	receive	a deeper and more lustrous colour from the sun…
the boy	was	so light-eyed and light-haired	that	the self-same rays	appeared to	draw out of him	what little colour he ever possessed.

Following this, provide a "just-in-time" mini-lesson on parallelism using the Parallelism and Coordination lesson from *Writing* book 1 to practice.

3. To reinforce students' understanding of this language area, return to a contextualized communicative activity (the whole), such as a Bridging Written Response activity. Students may target this language usage area in their writing and editing by choosing it as a goal on their Language Usage Checklist (p. 129).

4. To include parallelism (or proper coordination) in their writing, students can self-evaluate based on their new knowledge. They can identify areas where they have faulty parallelism or coordination and correct them or they can increase the complexity of their sentences and add parallelism and/or coordination.

➤ Assessment & Next Steps

Students should complete the suggested practice activities and the activities included in each lesson. Evaluate which learning goals were not met and remediate by using other resources, such as those identified in the "Bridging Knowledge" section. Upon successful completion, continue to the next lesson.

THEME

Skills-Based Questions

1. What is a theme and why is it important to understand the theme of a story?

2. How do you determine what the theme of a story is?

	Learning Goals:	GED
Knowledge Goals:	1. Draw conclusions about the theme of a story using text clues.	R.3.3
Reading Goals:	1. Determine the theme of a story and identify text clues that support it.	R.2.6
	2. Describe how elements of the text work together to develop the theme.	R.3.3
	3. Determine how parts of the text (words, phrases, clauses, and paragraphs) help develop the theme of the text.	R.5.1
Vocabulary Goals:	1. Define key subject and academic vocabulary.	R.4.1
	2. Determine the meaning of unknown vocabulary using context clues, word forms, and parts of speech.	
	3. Produce writing and speech using new vocabulary.	
Written Response Goals:	1. Draw conclusions about the theme of a story using text clues.	W.1
	2. Respond to text by describing its theme, organizing the writing to support this analysis, and focusing on the writing task.	W.2
	3. Use standard English language conventions. *(See Language Usage Goals)*	W.3
Language Usage Goals:	1. Identify and correct misplaced and dangling modifiers.	L.1.5
	2. Use capitalization correctly in writing.	L.2.1
	3. Edit writing to eliminate misplaced and dangling modifiers.	

Sample Instructional Support Strategies

➢ Bridging Knowledge

Strategy 1: *Develop prior knowledge and skills to connect to new knowledge.*

Strategy 2: *Use guiding questions to make connections beyond the lesson to broader life themes and topics.*

Strategy 3: *Use reading strategies to develop, monitor, and synthesize new knowledge.* (See Bridging Reading)

Strategy 4: *Demonstrate (and further develop) synthesis of new knowledge through written student response tasks.* (See Bridging Written Response)

1. Evaluate students' knowledge of the following language arts concepts and skills. Utilize the chart below to develop student background knowledge and skills as necessary.

Theme	Reading Theme	Writing Theme	Language Usage Misplaced and Dangling Modifiers
Writing for the GED Test Book 1: Grammar, Usage, and Mechanics			Misplaced Modifiers (p. 32); Dangling Modifiers (p. 34); Plurals and Possessives (p. 70)
Core Skills in Reading & Writing	Unit 1, Lesson 6: Theme (p. 28)	Unit 5, Lesson 1: Topic Sentences (p. 115); Lesson 2: Supporting Details (p. 118); Lesson 3: Transitions (p. 121)	
Scoreboost: Writing Across the Tests Sentence Structure, Usage, and Mechanics (SS); Responding to Text (RT)			SS: Use Modifiers Correctly (p. 12); Capitalize Correctly (p. 30)
Pre-HSE Workbook Reading (R); Writing 1 (W1); Writing 2 (W2)	R: Theme (p. 48)		W1: Capital Letters (p. 16)

2. Contextualize the GED Application portion of the lesson (p. 62) within a broader theme or topic by beginning the lesson with Guiding Questions. Guiding questions that are authentic and relevant to students draw them deeper into the lesson and allow them to build deeper knowledge beyond the content of the lesson.

Guiding Questions:

1. What is the theme of the excerpt from *The Little Match Girl*?

2. What does this theme suggest about the historical period in which Hans Christian Andersen wrote?

> ## Bridging Reading

Strategy 1: *Determine the type of text, establish reading purpose, and make predictions using text features and signal words.*

Strategy 2: *Develop text analysis using think-alouds, annotation, sentence frames, and graphic organizers.*

Strategy 3: *Overcome text analysis barriers using prior knowledge, analyzing language usage, and using resources.*

Strategy 4: *Synthesize text analysis using paraphrasing, text frames, graphic organizers, and peer discussions.*

1. Have students use pre-reading strategies (p. 8) to scan the text features and signal words to determine the type of text, its purpose, the purpose of the reading task (test prompt or question), and make predictions about the text. In order to not give away the ending, do not have students read the strategy questions at this time. A graphic organizer may be helpful for noting this information.

Example: Guided Practice (p. 60), excerpt from *The Oval Portrait*

	Answers	Text Features	Signal Words
Text Type	Short story excerpt	Title, quotations on title	excerpt
Text Purpose	To tell a story about a portrait	Title	Portrait
Reading Purpose	Answer questions about the conflict and theme of the story	the directions, the graphic organizer	conflict, theme
Prediction	There is a conflict between husband and wife about a portrait.	Title, graphic organizer	Portrait, "conflict between husband and wife"

2. The lesson's introduction (p. 59) provides a concept map with the kinds of text clues one can look for when determining the theme of a story. The Guided Practice provides a graphic organizer in which to write examples from the text about one of these categories of text clues, the conflict. A combination of the two graphic organizers, will allow students to really explore the categories of thematic clues, text examples that represent these categories, and conclusions drawn about the theme from these examples. In groups of three, have each student find a text example for one of the three thematic clue categories. They can then pool their information to complete the Lesson Learned? column. This will give them the main theme of the story.

	Characters	Conflicts	Outcome	Lesson Learned?
Text Example	Wife: "a maiden of rarest beauty…all light and smiles, and frolicsome…" Husband: "He, passionate, studious, austere, and having already a bride in his Art."	"[she] loving and cherishing all things; hating only the Art which was her rival… It was thus a terrible thing for this lady to hear the painter speak of his desire to portray even his young bride"	"'This is indeed Life itself'…She was dead!"	Reader: The husband valued Art more than his wife. He valued the unreal more than the real.
Theme	Be careful if you marry your opposite.	You can't change a person's character.	If you love something more than life, you may lose that life.	Be careful what you value. Life is more important than its reflection.

3. Although each story has its own theme, there are themes that commonly occur throughout fictional texts. Provide a list of these themes to help your students determine the theme for a story. If the theme for the story they are reading is not included on the list, they can add it for future reference. Here are some themes that are quite common.

> **Common Themes:** Good wins over evil; Value (cherish) life, people, the environment, etc.; Strength and courage help you succeed; Faith helps you overcome; Family (loyalty) is the most important thing in life; There is more to life than money; Honesty (integrity, respect, etc.) is the measure of a person; "What goes around comes around;" Hard work pays off.

4. Continuing with the group work from Strategy 2, have students state their conclusion about the story's theme and support it with examples from the text. They can use a paragraph frame to help them.

> **Example: Guided Practice, excerpt from *The Oval Portrait***
>
> *The theme of ___(name of story)___ is ___(state theme)___. Several examples ___(finish topic sentence)___. For instance, the characters ___(describe the characters)___. For example, in the text it says _____. Because the characters _____, there is a conflict over ___(describe the conflict)___. For example, the text says _____. At the end of the story, ___(describe the outcome of the conflict)___. This illustrates that _____. Therefore, ___(restate theme here)___.*

> ## Bridging Vocabulary

> **Strategy 1:** *Identify the component parts and usage of new words to interpret their meanings.*
>
> **Strategy 2:** *Use context clues to interpret new words, including figurative and connotative language.*
>
> **Strategy 3:** *Utilize vocabulary-building resources.*
>
> **Strategy 4:** *Build a deeper knowledge of words through writing and speaking tasks.*

1. First, present the shortest form of the word (the base word, often the verb form), followed by other commonly used word forms (if available). Examine prefixes and suffixes and their impact on word meaning and usage.

2. Read the word as used in the context of the text and discuss possible meanings given context clues and word form.

3. Have students find (electronically or in print) the definition or translation of the base form and, if different, the form used in context and note these definitions for future reference and study.

4. Gradually build a deeper knowledge of the word by having students use the word in a sentence frame, guided discussion, and an original sentence (see Appendix D, p. 144).

➤ Bridging Written Response

Strategy 1: *Prepare for a response task by identifying its purpose, audience, signal words, structure, and style.*

Strategy 2: *Organize text analysis for a written response using a graphic organizer and/or paragraph/essay frame.*

Strategy 3: *Overcome barriers to producing clear/coherent writing by using models, language analysis, and resources.*

Strategy 4: *Revise writing by utilizing peer- and self-editing checklists, rubrics, and writing resources.*

Strategy 5: *Extend text analysis to build upon initial information or claims by using evidence from additional sources.*

1. To prepare for the response task, students need to identify the writing purpose (based on the writing prompt), the language they will use to meet their purpose (the signal words), and the area of language usage on which they will focus (Language Usage Goals). The graphic organizer below may help students with this preparation.

Task: Write a paragraph describing the theme of the excerpt from *The Little Match Girl*. Support your conclusions with examples about the characters, conflict, and outcome of the story.

Response Type	Present conclusions
Writing Purpose	Write a paragraph sharing conclusions about the theme of the story. Include examples from the text about the characters and conflict to support it.
Signal Words	*Conclusion:* therefore, thus, in conclusion, as such, given, for this reason *Examples:* for example, such as, including, one example is, for instance, to illustrate *Demonstrate:* shows, illustrates, represents, reflects, demonstrates
Language Usage Goal	*Student chooses a language usage area on which to focus.*

2. Students can use the paragraph frame from Bridging Reading Strategy 4 (or one like it) to develop their response to the task above.

3. In Bridging Reading, students completed a paragraph in small groups describing the theme of the excerpt from *The Oval Portrait*. Use that paragraph as a model for completion of this Bridging Written Response task.

4. A simple rubric can help students prepare for, compose, and revise their writing. Students can develop the rubric with your help based on the task directions. For example, given the task above, students are required to do three things: 1) write a paragraph; 2) make conclusions about the theme of the story; 3) support conclusions with examples from different categories of thematic clues. A rubric should also describe three or more levels of competency. Decide with your students how to label these levels. Here is an example of a rubric you may develop:

Low	Developing	Sufficient	Strong
Does not state a conclusion.	States an unclear or unsupported conclusion.	States a somewhat supported conclusion about the theme of *The Little Match Girl*.	States a well-supported conclusion about the theme of *The Little Match Girl*.
Does not provide appropriate examples.	Provides supporting examples from one of the following: characters, conflict, or outcome of the story.	Provides supporting examples from two of the following: characters, conflict, or outcome of the story.	Provides supporting examples about all three of following: the characters, conflict, and outcome of the story.
Does not use any elements of correct paragraph structure.	Uses one element of correct paragraph structure.	Uses two elements of correct paragraph structure.	Uses correct paragraph structure: topic sentence, supporting details, and concluding sentence.

5. The guiding question "What does this theme suggest about the historical period in which Hans Christian Andersen wrote?" provides students the opportunity to extend their knowledge of the theme of *The Little Match Girl* to mid-19th century European history and art. From the Irish potato famine to Victorian art and literature, the theme allows students to look at the stark contrast between the classes, its representation in art and literature, and even make comparisons to the issues of today.

➢ Bridging Language Usage

Strategy 1:	*Determine and target areas of language usage that require further development.*
Strategy 2:	*Analyze specific areas of language usage as modeled in authentic and relevant communication tasks.*
Strategy 3:	*Develop specific areas of language usage through participation in authentic communication tasks.*
Strategy 4:	*Revise language usage by utilizing peer- and self-editing checklists, rubrics, and language resources.*

1. Determine the language needs of the students and choose a particular language usage area to focus on for this lesson. As an example, let's focus on the correct use of modifiers. (Another language focus suggested for this lesson is proper use of plurals and possessives.)

2. Since it is hardly likely that you will find errors in the use of modifiers in established literature, use examples of student writing from the Bridging Reading Strategy 4 activity. If no authentic examples emerge, create a few of your own from the activity or rewrite some sentences from one of the readings in this lesson. There is the potential for great humor here (but not necessarily given our current themes!). Here are a couple of examples.

> ***Misplaced Modifier:*** He looked at the picture of his wife he painted.
> *Ask:* What in the story did he paint? What in the sentence did he paint? The picture? Or his wife?
>
> ***Dangling Modifier:*** Finishing the painting, his wife was dead.
> *Ask:* Who finished the painting in the story? Who finished the painting in this sentence? How can we fix it?

Following this, provide a "just-in-time" mini-lesson on correcting misplaced and dangling modifiers using the Misplaced Modifiers and Dangling Modifiers lessons from *Writing* book 1.

3. To reinforce students' understanding of this language area, return to a contextualized communicative activity (the whole), such as a Bridging Written Response activity. Students may target this language usage area in their writing and editing by choosing it as a goal on their Language Usage Checklist (p. 129).

4. Have students check their use of modifiers by asking, "What or whom does the modifier describe?" Students need to move misplaced modifiers next to the word(s) they describe. For dangling modifiers, students need to add the word (or words) that are being described.

➢ Assessment & Next Steps

Students should complete the suggested practice activities and the activities included in each lesson. Evaluate which learning goals were not met and remediate by using other resources, such as those identified in the Bridging Knowledge section. Upon successful completion, continue to the next lesson.

FIGURATIVE LANGUAGE

Skills-Based Questions

1. What types of figurative language do authors use to tell their stories?

2. How do you interpret figurative language and what point does it make in the story?

	Learning Goals:	**GED**
Knowledge Goals:	1. Identify types of figurative language, and determine the meaning figurative language gives to the story.	R.4.1
		R.4.3
Reading Goals:	1. Interpret the meaning of figurative language.	R.4.1
	2. Describe how figurative language affects the message of the story.	R.4.3
Vocabulary Goals:	1. Define key subject and academic vocabulary.	R.4.1
	2. Determine the meaning of unknown vocabulary using context clues, word forms, and parts of speech.	
	3. Produce writing and speech using new vocabulary.	
Written Response Goals:	1. Interpret figurative language and describe how it affects the message of the story.	W.1
	2. Respond to text by describing its use of figurative language, organizing the writing to support this analysis, and focusing on the writing task.	W.2
		W.3
	3. Use standard English language conventions. *(See Language Usage Goals)*	
Language Usage Goals:	1. Identify and correct informal and nonstandard English.	L.1.4
	2. Identify and improve wordy and awkward sentences.	L.1.8
	3. Use words that sound alike correctly in writing.	L.1.1
	4. Edit writing to eliminate informal and nonstandard English and revise wordy and awkward sentences.	

Sample Instructional Support Strategies

➤ Bridging Knowledge

> **Strategy 1:** *Develop prior knowledge and skills to connect to new knowledge.*
>
> **Strategy 2:** *Use guiding questions to make connections beyond the lesson to broader life themes and topics.*
>
> **Strategy 3:** *Use reading strategies to develop, monitor, and synthesize new knowledge.* (See Bridging Reading)
>
> **Strategy 4:** *Demonstrate (and further develop) synthesis of new knowledge through written student response tasks.* (See Bridging Written Response)

1. Evaluate students' knowledge of the following language arts concepts and skills. Utilize the chart below to develop student background knowledge and skills as necessary.

Figurative Language	Reading Figurative Language	Writing Figurative Language	Language Usage Informal and Nonstandard Usage Wordy and Awkward Sentences
Writing for the GED Test Book 1: Grammar, Usage, and Mechanics			Informal and Nonstandard Usage (p. 58); Wordy and Awkward Writing (p. 60); Capitalization (p. 64); Words That Sound Alike (p. 72)
Core Skills in Reading & Writing	Unit 2, Lesson 3: Figurative Language in Poetry (p. 40)	Unit 5, Lesson 1: Topic Sentences (p. 115); Lesson 2: Supporting Details (p. 118); Lesson 3: Transitions (p. 121)	
Scoreboost: Writing Across the Tests Sentence Structure, Usage, and Mechanics (SS); Responding to Text (RT)			SS: Edit to Eliminate Wordy or Awkward Sentences (p. 16)
Pre-HSE Workbook Reading (R); Writing 1 (W1); Writing 2 (W2)	R: Figurative Language (p. 46)		

2. Contextualize the GED Application portion of the lesson (p. 68) within a broader theme or topic by beginning the lesson with Guiding Questions. Guiding questions that are authentic and relevant to students draw them deeper into the lesson and allow them to build deeper knowledge beyond the content of the lesson.

> **Guiding Questions:**
>
> 1. How does the figurative language used in *A Detail* emphasize the message of the story?
> 2. How does water, as described in this story, compare to the urban lifestyle?

➤ Bridging Reading

> **Strategy 1:** *Determine the type of text, establish reading purpose, and make predictions using text features and signal words.*
>
> **Strategy 2:** *Develop text analysis using think-alouds, annotation, sentence frames, and graphic organizers.*
>
> **Strategy 3:** *Overcome text analysis barriers using prior knowledge, analyzing language usage, and using resources.*
>
> **Strategy 4:** *Synthesize text analysis using paraphrasing, text frames, graphic organizers, and peer discussions.*

1. Have students use pre-reading strategies (p. 8) to scan the text features and signal words to determine the type of text, its purpose, the purpose of the reading task (test prompt or question), and to make predictions about the text. In order to not give away the ending, do not have students read the strategy questions at this time. A graphic organizer may be helpful for noting this information.

Example: Guided Practice (p. 66), excerpt from *The Most Dangerous Game*

	Answers	Text Features	Signal Words
Text Type	Short story excerpt	Title, quotations on title	excerpt
Text Purpose	To tell a story about a dangerous game	Title	Dangerous Game
Reading Purpose	Answer questions about the figurative language in the story	the directions, the graphic organizer	simile, hyperbole, metaphor, personification
Prediction	It's about a dangerous game	Title	Dangerous Game

2. The lesson introduction (p. 64) provides a concept map with steps to interpret figurative language and determine what point it makes in the story. The Guided Practice provides a graphic organizer to write examples from the text of three kinds of figurative language. A combination of the two graphic organizers, will allow students to identify text examples of each kind of figurative language used in the text, interpret these examples, and determine how they affect the message of the story. In groups of four, have each student look for a text example for one of four kinds of figurative language. Then they can pool their information.

	Simile	Metaphor	Personification	Hyperbole
Step 1: Text Example	"It's like moist black velvet."	"What I felt was a–a mental chill."	"dank tropical night… pressed its thick warm blackness in upon the yacht."	"who'd go up to the devil himself and ask him for a light."
Step 2: Similarities	Heavy, thick, black	Makes you shiver	Heavy, thick, black	Not afraid of anything
Step 3: The Message	Calm before a storm, ominous	Fear, dread	Calm before a storm, ominous	Emphasizes that he's afraid of the island

3. In order for ELLs to be successful with the above activity, they may need extra support to both understand the literal meaning behind the figurative one and the intended figurative meaning. Providing a reference sheet with some of this figurative language may be helpful. Or have students identify confusing areas of the text and help them define the literal meanings and interpret the figurative meanings. To extend students' vocabulary, have them use a thesaurus to find synonyms of these words and note the connotations in parentheses.

Figurative language	Translation/Definition	Synonym	Synonym
moist, black *velvet* ↑ ↑ (seems humid) (heavy fabric)	*Student translates or defines these words*	wet (neutral)	dank (moist and maybe smelly like mold)
mental *chill* ↑ (deep, sudden cold)	*Student translates or defines these words*	cold (neutral)	shiver (a chill that moves your body)

4. Continuing with the group work from Strategy 2, have students use the text example they added to the chart and construct sentences that define what kind of figurative language their example is, the similarity it expresses, and how it affects the meaning of the story.

Example: Guided Practice, excerpt from *The Dangerous Game*

One example of a simile from the text is "It's like moist black velvet." This simile shows how the night is wet, thick, and black like the velvet. It gives the story an ominous feeling like the calm before a storm.

Students can then put the sentences from everyone in the group together and create a topic sentence and concluding sentence to make a complete paragraph.

➢ Bridging Vocabulary

> **Strategy 1:** *Identify the component parts and usage of new words to interpret their meanings.*
>
> **Strategy 2:** *Use context clues to interpret new words, including figurative and connotative language.*
>
> **Strategy 3:** *Utilize vocabulary-building resources.*
>
> **Strategy 4:** *Build a deeper knowledge of words through writing and speaking tasks.*

1. First, present the shortest form of the word (the base word, often the verb form), followed by other commonly used word forms (if available). Examine prefixes and suffixes and their impact on word meaning and usage.

2. Read the word as used in the context of the text and discuss possible meanings given context clues and word form.

3. Have students find (electronically or in print) the definition or translation of the base form and, if different, the form used in context and note these definitions for future reference and study.

4. Gradually build a deeper knowledge of the word by having students use the word in a sentence frame, guided discussion, and an original sentence (see Appendix D, p. 144).

➢ Bridging Written Response

> **Strategy 1:** *Prepare for a response task by identifying its purpose, audience, signal words, structure, and style.*
>
> **Strategy 2:** *Organize text analysis for written response using a graphic organizer and/or paragraph/essay frame.*
>
> **Strategy 3:** *Overcome barriers to producing clear/coherent writing by using models, language analysis, and resources.*
>
> **Strategy 4:** *Revise writing by utilizing peer- and self-editing checklists, rubrics, and writing resources.*
>
> Strategy 5:   *Extend text analysis to build upon initial information or claims by using evidence from additional sources.*

1. To prepare for the response task, students need to identify the writing purpose (based on the writing prompt), the language they will use to meet their purpose (the signal words), and the area of language usage on which they will focus (Language Usage Goal). The graphic organizer below may help students with this preparation.

Task: Write a paragraph describing how the figurative language in *The Detail* affects the meaning of the story. Use examples of figurative language from the text and state what kind of figurative language it is.

Response Type	Present conclusions
Writing Purpose	Write a paragraph sharing conclusions about how figurative language affects the meaning of the story. Include text examples of different kinds of figurative language.
Signal Words	*Comparison:* likewise, similarly, same as, like, similar to, equally *Examples:* for example, such as, including, one example is, for instance, to illustrate *Demonstrate:* shows, illustrates, represents, reflects, demonstrates *Conclusion:* therefore, thus, in conclusion, as such, given, for this reason
Language Usage Goal	*Student chooses a language usage area on which to focus.*

2. Students can use the paragraph frame from Bridging Reading Strategy 4 (or one like it) to develop their response to the task above.

3. In Bridging Reading, students completed a paragraph in small groups describing the theme of the excerpt from *The Oval Portrait*. Work with students to revise these paragraphs to include the signal words needed for a clear coherent paragraph. This provides a model for the Bridging Written Response task.

4. As in previous lessons, a simple rubric can help students prepare for, compose, and revise their writing. Used in conjunction with peer editing, this is a powerful way for students to be held accountable for understanding the task and meeting its requirements. For this task, students are required to do four things: 1) write a paragraph; 2) make conclusions about how figurative language affects the meaning of the story; 3) support conclusions with examples from different kinds of figurative language; and 4) identify the kinds of figurative language used in the examples.

Low	Developing	Sufficient	Strong
Does not state a conclusion.	States an unclear or unsupported conclusion about the figurative language's affect on the story's meaning.	States a somewhat supported conclusion about how figurative language affects the meaning of the story.	States a well-supported conclusion about how figurative language affects the meaning of the story.
Does not provide appropriate examples.	Provides supporting examples of one of following: simile, metaphor, personification, and hyperbole.	Provides supporting examples of two of following: simile, metaphor, personification, and hyperbole.	Provides supporting examples of three of following: simile, metaphor, personification, and hyperbole.
Does not correctly identify the kind of figurative language.	Correctly identifies the kind of figurative language used in one example.	Correctly identifies the kind of figurative language used in two examples.	Correctly identifies the kind of figurative language used in each example.
Does not use any elements of correct paragraph structure.	Uses one element of correct paragraph structure.	Uses two elements of correct paragraph structure.	Uses correct paragraph structure: Topic sentence, supporting details, and concluding sentence.

➤ Bridging Language Usage

Strategy 1: *Determine and target areas of language usage that require further development.*

Strategy 2: *Analyze specific areas of language usage as modeled in authentic and relevant communication tasks.*

Strategy 3: *Develop specific areas of language usage through participation in authentic communication tasks.*

Strategy 4: *Revise language usage by utilizing peer- and self-editing checklists, rubrics, and language resources.*

1. Determine the language needs of the students and choose a particular language usage area to focus on for this lesson. As an example, let's focus on wordy and awkward sentences. (Eliminating informal and nonstandard English, capitalization, and homophones are also suggested areas of focus for this lesson).

2. Fictional texts often provide lengthy, colorful, and creative descriptions. Students should not mistake these kinds of descriptions for "wordy." Emphasize how wordiness will depend on the purpose of the text. Informational texts will be much more concise. However, wordiness is still an issue with fiction when it includes redundancy and inconsequential information. Especially in writing poetry and short stories, authors pride themselves in retaining only words that are essential to crafting the elements of their poem or story. Have students analyze a passage from the readings in this lesson. Ask them why the author chose to keep the words he did. What if they cut out something? How would it change the story? Following this, provide a mini-lesson using the Wordy and Awkward Writing lesson from *Writing* book 1.

3. To reinforce students understanding of this language area, return to a contextualized communicative activity (the whole), such as a Bridging Written Response activity. Students may target this language usage area in their writing and editing by choosing it as a goal on their Language Usage Checklist (p. 129).

4. Have students check wordiness of their writing by asking: "What is not needed to meet the requirements of the assignment?" "What is not needed to support my conclusions?" "Can I say this in a more concise way?"

➤ Assessment & Next Steps

Students should complete the suggested practice activities and the activities included in each lesson. Evaluate which learning goals were not met and remediate by using other resources, such as those identified in the Bridging Knowledge section. Upon successful completion, continue to the Cumulative Review.

Introduction to Extended Response

EXTENDED-RESPONSE ITEMS / EXTENDED-RESPONSE RUBRIC

Skills-Based Questions

1. What does the extended response item on the GED test contain and how do you make sure to understand it?

2. What do you need to include for a strong extended response and how can you evaluate it?

	Learning Goals:	GED (NA)
Knowledge Goals:	1. Identify the parts of the extended-response item on the GED test.	
	2. Identify criteria for writing a strong extended response.	
Reading Goals:	1. Recognize the parts of the extended-response item on the GED test.	
	2. "Unpack" the extended-response writing prompt.	
	3. Identify the three steps in writing an extended response.	
Vocabulary Goals:	1. Define key test-taking vocabulary.	
Written Response Goals:	NA	
Language Usage Goals:	1. Identify the verbs and objects in the writing prompt and rubric that describe the requirements of the extended response.	

Sample Instructional Support Strategies

➢ **Bridging Knowledge: Not Applicable.**

This lesson provides the background knowledge and skills necessary to understand how to complete the extended-response item on the GED test.

➢ Bridging Reading

Strategy 1: *Determine the type of text, establish reading purpose, and make predictions using text features and signal words.*

Strategy 2: *Develop text analysis using think-alouds, annotation, sentence frames, and graphic organizers.*

Strategy 3: *Overcome text analysis barriers using prior knowledge, analyzing language usage, and using resources.*

Strategy 4: *Synthesize text analysis using paraphrasing, text frames, graphic organizers, and peer discussions.*

1. Ask students to scan the extended response example on page 6 of the lesson in *Writing* book 3 and analyze each part of the extended-response item. Then have students define each component, describe its purpose, and give an example of it from the text.

	Passage	Prompt	Writing Box
Definition	*a nonfiction reading selection*		
Purpose	*to present an argument we must evaluate*		
Example	*"Editorial: Don't Label Genetically Modified Foods"*		

Regarding the lesson on the extended response rubric, ask students to read all three traits and then ask them about the purpose of the rubric. What is the rubric intended for? How can it help them with their extended response?

2. Have students read the writing prompt on page 6 and ask themselves, "What am I supposed to do?" On the erasable noteboard like the one they will be provided during the test, have students jot down what the *action* is, *what* is to be accomplished, and *how* and/or *why* it is to be accomplished. Given the example from page 7, annotations may look like this:

Action	What?	How or Why?
Analyze	the editorial and letter	to determine which is stronger
Use	relevant and specific evidence	from both sources to support response
Type	response	in the box (45 minutes)

For the rubric, students should note the three steps to complete the extended response as well as each step's important components.

Step 1:	Step 2:	Step 3:
•	•	•
•	•	•
•		•

3. ELLs can pursue this "unpacking" further by underlining the verbs twice and their objects and conditions once. This will help clarify what the action is, what is to be accomplished, and how and/or why it is to be accomplished.

Action	What?	How or Why?
Analyze	the editorial and letter	to determine which is stronger
Use	relevant and specific evidence	from both sources to support response
Type	response	in the box (45 minutes)

For the rubric, concentrate on "unpacking" these requirements as well by underlining the verbs twice and their objects and conditions once.

Create an argument using evidence
- Follow prompt directions
- Evaluate the argument
- State your side and why
- Use examples from the passages to support your side

➢ Bridging Vocabulary

Strategy 1: *Identify the component parts and usage of new words to interpret their meanings.*

Strategy 2: *Use context clues to interpret new words, including figurative and connotative language.*

Strategy 3: *Utilize vocabulary-building resources* (for lesson, not for test).

Strategy 4: *Build a deeper knowledge of words through writing and speaking tasks* (for lesson, not for test).

1. First, present the shortest form of the word (the base word, often the verb form), followed by other commonly used word forms (if available). Examine prefixes and suffixes and their impact on word meaning and usage.

2. Read the word as used in the context of the text and discuss possible meanings given context clues and word form.

3. Have students find (electronically or in print) the definition or translation of the base form and, if different, the form used in context and note these definitions for future reference and study *(for lesson, not for test)*.

4. Gradually build a deeper knowledge of the word by having students use the word in a sentence frame, guided discussion, and an original sentence (see Appendix D, p. 144) *(for lesson, not for test.)*

➢ Bridging Written Response: *Not Applicable*

This lesson focuses on the skills of reading and understanding an extended response prompt and rubric as focused on in the above Bridging Reading section.

➢ Bridging Language Usage: *Not Applicable*

Although this lesson will require students to identify verbs and objects, it is too short to merit use of strategies. Simply provide extra instruction on identifying verbs and objects in sentences.

➢ Assessment & Next Steps

Students should complete the suggested practice activities and the activities included in each lesson. Evaluate which learning goals were not met and remediate by using other resources, such as those identified in the Bridging Knowledge section. Upon successful completion, continue to the next lesson.

Read and Analyze

ANALYZING ARGUMENTS

Skills-Based Questions

1. What is a claim and how do you know if it is valid?

2. How does a writer create a strong argument?

	Learning Goals:	GED
Knowledge Goals:	1. Identify the parts of an argument and how they work together to support a claim.	R.8.1
Reading Goals:	1. Determine the author's claim, the points in his/her argument, and how they build on one another to support the claim.	R.8.1
		R.8.2
	2. Identify evidence the author uses to support a claim or conclusion.	R.5.4
	3. Determine how a section of the text affects meaning or supports the author's purpose.	
Vocabulary Goals:	1. Define key subject and academic vocabulary.	R.4.1
	2. Determine the meaning of unknown vocabulary using context clues, word forms, and parts of speech.	
	3. Produce writing and speech using new vocabulary.	
Written Response Goals:	1. Summarize the central claims, supporting evidence, and counterarguments of the text.	W.1
	2. Use standard English language conventions. *(See Language Usage Goals)*	W.3
Language Usage Goals:	1. Identify subject and predicate and correct subject/predicate order.	L.1.5
	2. Edit writing to include complete sentences with correct subject/predicate order.	L.1.6

Sample Instructional Support Strategies

➤ Bridging Knowledge

Strategy 1: *Develop prior knowledge and skills to connect to new knowledge.*

Strategy 2: *Use guiding questions to make connections beyond the lesson to broader life themes and topics.*

Strategy 3: *Use reading strategies to develop, monitor, and synthesize new knowledge.* (See Bridging Reading)

Strategy 4: *Demonstrate (and further develop) synthesis of new knowledge through written student response tasks.*

1. Evaluate students' knowledge of the following language arts concepts and skills. Utilize the chart below to develop student background knowledge and skills as necessary.

Analyzing Arguments	Reading Analyzing Arguments	Writing Analyzing Arguments	Language Usage Sentence Structure
Writing for the GED Test Book 1: Grammar, Usage, and Mechanics			Simple and Compound Sentences (p. 22); Sentence Fragments (p. 26); Run-ons and Comma Splices (p. 28)
Core Skills in Reading & Writing	Unit 6, Lesson 1: Types of Essays (p. 126)	Unit 5, Lesson 1: Topic Sentences (p. 115); Lesson 2: Supporting Details (p. 118); Lesson 3: Transitions (p. 121)	Unit 4, Lesson 2: Sentence Structure (p. 84); Lesson 3: Types of Sentences (p. 88); Lesson 7: Capitalization (p. 102)
Scoreboost: Writing Across the Tests Sentence Structure, Usage, and Mechanics (SS); Responding to Text (RT)	RT: Analyze Arguments in Text (p. 4); Collect Supporting Details in Text (p. 7)		SS: Correct Sentence Fragments (p. 10); Correct Run-Ons and Fused Sentences (p. 4)
Scoreboost: Thinking Skills Critical Thinking	Determine the Purpose of a Text (p. 34)		
Pre-HSE Workbook Reading (R); Writing 1 (W1); Writing 2 (W2)	R: Text Types and Purposes (p. 18); Arguments (p. 32)	W2: Arguments (p. 24); Paragraph structure (pp. 12–22)	W1: Parts of a Sentence (p. 12); Sentence Fragments (p. 42); Complete Sentences (p. 34); Run-Ons and Comma Splices (p. 40)

2. Contextualize the Guided Practice portion of the lesson (p. 14) within a broader theme or topic by beginning the lesson with Guiding Questions. Guiding questions that are authentic and relevant to students draw them deeper into the lesson and allow them to build deeper knowledge beyond the content of the lesson.

Guiding Questions:

1. What is the author's claim about wind power in the article and what evidence does he/she give to support it?

2. What are the counterarguments against wind power and how does the author refute them?

➤ Bridging Reading

Strategy 1: *Determine the type of text, establish reading purpose, and make predictions using text features and signal words.*

Strategy 2: *Develop text analysis using think-alouds, annotation, sentence frames, and graphic organizers.*

Strategy 3: *Overcome text analysis barriers using prior knowledge, analyzing language usage, and using resources.*

Strategy 4: *Synthesize text analysis using paraphrasing, text frames, graphic organizers, and peer discussions.*

1. For the extended-response item on the GED test, students will need to prepare for their response by "unpacking" the writing prompt, understanding the purpose of the reading passages, and making predictions about the claim the argument will make. Here is an example of how to use a graphic organizer to help ELLs understand the directions in a writing prompt and gives them extra practice in preparing for their response.

Writing prompt directions: *In your response, summarize the parts of the argument, such as the central claim, supporting evidence, and counterarguments. Use text examples to demonstrate each part of the argument.*		
Action Summarize Use	**What?** the parts of the argument: claim, supporting evidence, and counterarguments examples	**How or Why?** from the text to demonstrate them
Text Purpose	*Argument/to persuade*	
Prediction	*Supports the use of wind power*	

2. Analysis consists of identifying the central claim, supporting evidence, and counterarguments (along with any refutation). The strategies in the margin of the Guided Practice provide annotation practice for students by asking them to underline these components as they identify them in the text. A graphic organizer can help students isolate these further.

Claim:

Evidence:	Evidence:	Evidence:	Counterargument:

3. Since ELLs will not be able to use resources to help them understand the passages on the GED test, it is best if they do not use Bridging Reading Strategy 3 when they practice for the extended response. Instead, after they identify language they do not understand in the passage, have them use a five-step process to figure out confusing areas (see flowchart below):

   1. Read the sentence for gist: who, where, when, what (are they doing/is happening/is the problem/ etc.)

   2. Read the cluster of sentences (phrases or clauses) around the word/phrase and use context clues

   3. Determine the part of speech of the unknown word(s)

   4. Study each word's base/prefix/suffix

   5. Use the context of the complete passage to "guess" at the meaning.

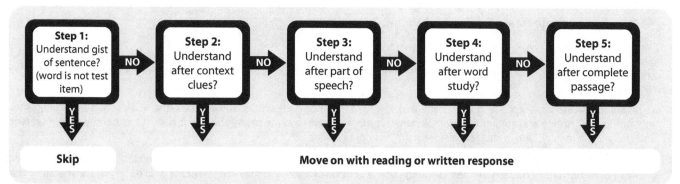

4. Have students answer the writing prompt from Strategy 2 using the information they added to the graphic organizer. A paragraph frame such as this one may guide them in this process.

The central claim of the argument is _____. The writer gives several reasons _____. One reason is _____. Another reason is _____. Finally, the writer says _____. The writer also presents the counterargument that _____. The writer refutes this argument when he says _____.

➢ Bridging Vocabulary

> **Strategy 1: *Identify the component parts and usage of new words to interpret their meanings.***
>
> **Strategy 2: *Use context clues to interpret new words, including figurative and connotative language.***
>
> Strategy 3: *Utilize vocabulary-building resources. (Not recommended for extended response practice.)*
>
> **Strategy 4: *Build a deeper knowledge of words through writing and speaking tasks.***

1. First, present the shortest form of the word (the base word, often the verb form), followed by other commonly used word forms (if available). Examine prefixes and suffixes and their impact on word meaning and usage.

2. Read the word as used in the context of the text and discuss possible meanings given context clues and word form.

4. Gradually build a deeper knowledge of the word by having students use the word in a sentence frame, guided discussion, and an original sentence (see Appendix D, p. 144).

➢ Bridging Written Response: *Not Applicable*

This lesson focuses on the skills of reading and text analysis (Trait 1 of the Extended Response Rubric for the GED test) and is therefore covered within the above Bridging Reading section.

➢ Bridging Language Usage

> **Strategy 1: *Determine and target areas of language usage that require further development.***
>
> **Strategy 2: *Analyze specific areas of language usage as modeled in authentic and relevant communication tasks.***
>
> **Strategy 3: *Develop specific areas of language usage through participation in authentic communication tasks.***
>
> **Strategy 4: *Revise language usage by utilizing peer- and self-editing checklists, rubrics, and language resources.***

1. Although minimal writing is required to synthesize the reading for this lesson, continued vigilance in monitoring ELLs' language usage is critical. Given the Bridging Reading tasks above, have students choose a language usage goal to focus on and mark it on their Language Usage Checklist (p. 129). Or, as the teacher, you may determine the language needs of the students. As an example, for this lesson let's focus on Sentence Structure (p. 36) within the Check and Revise unit of *Writing* book 3.

2. Analyze examples from the reading or from the synthesis task that demonstrate the chosen language area, such as sentence structure. For example, pull simple sentences from the text and dissect the sentences for subject, verb (include negatives but explain they are adverbs), and phrases.

> (In fact), <u>coal</u> <u>is</u> the biggest single air polluter (in the United States).
>
> <u>Energy companies</u> <u>do not install</u> just one turbine (here and there).

Finally, provide a "just-in-time" mini-lesson using the Sentence Structure lesson (p. 36) to give students more practice with analyzing this language area.

3. To reinforce development of the language usage area, return to the Bridging Reading synthesis task (the whole) and have students target this area in their writing and editing. For example, when students are filling in the paragraph frame, have them identify simple sentences and check them for inclusion of subject and verb.

4. When the writing is complete, students can self and/or peer edit using the Editing Rubric (p. 131). Once this language goal is mastered, they can write the date of mastery on their Language Usage Checklist. Otherwise, they can revisit the goal during the next writing task.

➢ Assessment & Next Steps

Students should complete the suggested practice activities and the activities included in each lesson. Evaluate which learning goals were not met and remediate by using other resources, such as those identified in the Bridging Knowledge section. Upon successful completion, continue to the next lesson.

EVALUATING REASONING

Skills-Based Questions

1. How do you know if an argument is weak or strong?

2. How do you evaluate its reasons and evidence?

	Learning Goals:	**GED**
Knowledge Goals:	1. Identify the types of reasons that build strong arguments.	R.8.1
	2. Identify the types of evidence that build strong reasoning.	
Reading Goals:	1. Evaluate how well the author supports his or her claim.	R.8.3
	2. Determine which claims are supported by evidence and which are not.	R.8.4
	3. Determine if the reasoning in an argument is valid and how false reasoning affects the argument.	R.8.5 R.9.3
	4. Compare and contrast how two texts on the same topic support their arguments.	
Vocabulary Goals:	1. Define key subject and academic vocabulary.	R.4.1
	2. Determine the meaning of unknown vocabulary using context clues, word forms, and parts of speech.	
	3. Produce writing and speech using new vocabulary.	
Written Response Goals:	1. Determine the weakness or strength of an article.	W.1
	2. State a claim about the weakness or strength of an argument and support it with evidence from the text.	W.2 W.3
	3. Use standard English language conventions. *(See Language Usage Goals)*	
Language Usage Goals:	1. Identify simple, compound, and complex sentences and use them correctly in writing.	L.1.6
	2. Edit writing to include compound sentences with appropriate conjunctions and complex sentences with appropriate transition words and punctuation.	L.2.2 L.1.9

Sample Instructional Support Strategies

➤ **Bridging Knowledge**

> **Strategy 1:** *Develop prior knowledge and skills to connect to new knowledge.*
>
> **Strategy 2:** *Use guiding questions to make connections beyond the lesson to broader life themes and topics.*
>
> **Strategy 3:** *Use reading strategies to develop, monitor, and synthesize new knowledge.* (See "Bridging Reading")

1. Evaluate students' knowledge of the following language arts concepts and skills. Utilize the chart below to develop student background knowledge and skills as necessary.

Evaluating Reasoning	Reading Evaluating Reasoning	Writing Evaluating Reasoning	Language Usage Sentence Variety
Writing for the GED Test Book 1: Grammar, Usage, and Mechanics			Simple and Compound Sentences (p. 22); Complex Sentences (p. 24)
Core Skills in Reading & Writing	Unit 6, Lesson 1: Types of Essays (p. 126)	Unit 5, Lesson 1: Topic Sentences (p. 115); Lesson 2: Supporting Details (p. 118); Lesson 3: Transitions (p. 121)	Unit 4, Lesson 2: Sentence Structure (p. 84); Lesson 3: Types of Sentences (p. 88); Lesson 7: Capitalization (p. 102)
Scoreboost: Writing Across the Tests Sentence Structure, Usage, and Mechanics (SS); Responding to Text (RT)	RT: Analyze Arguments in Text (p. 4); Collect Supporting Details in Text (p. 7)		SS: Coordinate Ideas in Sentences (p. 6); Subordinate Ideas in Sentences (p. 8)
Scoreboost: Thinking Skills Critical Thinking	Differentiate Facts from Opinion and Speculation (p. 30); Evaluate Relevance and Sufficiency of Information (p. 32)		
Pre-HSE Workbook Reading (R); Writing 1 (W1); Writing 2 (W2)	R: Arguments (p. 32); Credibility (p. 34); Reasoning (p. 36)	W2: Evaluate Arguments (p. 36); Paragraph structure (pp. 12–22)	W1: Compound Sentences (p. 36); Complex Sentences (p. 38); Sentence Variety (p. 46)

2. Contextualize the Guided Practice portion of the lesson (p. 18) within a broader theme or topic by beginning the lesson with Guiding Questions. Guiding questions that are authentic and relevant to students draw them deeper into the lesson and allow them to build deeper knowledge beyond the content of the lesson.

> **Guiding Questions:**
>
> 1. What is the writer's claim about a solution to "Our Energy Dilemma," and what evidence does he/she give to support it?
>
> 2. What are the strengths and weaknesses of the writer's use of reasoning and evidence?

> ## Bridging Reading

Strategy 1: *Determine the type of text, establish reading purpose, and make predictions using text features and signal words.*

Strategy 2: *Develop text analysis using think-alouds, annotation, sentence frames, and graphic organizers.*

Strategy 3: *Overcome text analysis barriers using prior knowledge, analyzing language usage, and using resources.*

Strategy 4: *Synthesize text analysis using paraphrasing, text frames, graphic organizers, and peer discussions.*

1. For the extended-response item on the GED test, students will need to prepare for their response by "unpacking" the writing prompt, understanding the purpose of the reading passages, and making predictions about the claims and validity of the argument. Here is an example of how to use a graphic organizer to help ELLs understand the directions in a writing prompt and gives them extra practice in preparing for their response.

Writing prompt directions: *In your response, state a claim about the strength of the argument, for example, is it strong, somewhat strong, or weak. Describe the strong and weak points of the argument using text examples. Make sure to explain why a point is strong or weak using knowledge of fallacies of logic and faulty reasoning.*

Action	What?	How or Why?
State	a claim about the strength of the argument	strong, somewhat strong, weak
Describe	strong and weak points	using text examples
Explain	why it is weak or strong	using knowledge of fallacies of logic and faulty reasoning

Text Purpose	*Argument/to persuade*
Prediction	*Supports energy conservation by using "green" buildings*

2. When evaluating an argument, first analyze it for its component parts (central claim, supporting evidence, and counterarguments) and then evaluate the argument for specific, relevant, and sound reasoning and reliable evidence. The strategies in the margin of the Guided Practice provide annotation practice for students by asking them to underline these components as they identify them in the text. Filling out a graphic organizer with evaluation criteria can guide students in evaluating each component. During the GED test, students will not have access to this checklist, but they can jot what they remember on the erasable noteboard in a similar fashion.

Claim:				
	Evidence	**Evidence**	**Evidence**	**Counterargument**
Text Examples:				
• Relevant & specific?				
• Sufficient?				
• Sound logic? (No? Circle below*)				
• Reliable evidence? (No? Circle below**)				
Fallacies of Logic: 1) Jump on the Bandwagon 2) Personal Attack 3) Either/Or Thinking 4) Slippery Slope				
**Unreliable Evidence: 1) not knowledgeable source 2) biased source 3) outdated information*				

3. Since ELLs will not be able to use resources to help them understand the passages on the GED test, it is best if they do not use Bridging Reading Strategy 3 when they practice for the extended response. Instead, after they identify language they do not understand in the passage, have them use a five-step process to figure out confusing areas (see flowchart on the next page):

   1. Read the sentence for gist: who, where, when, what (are they doing/is happening/is the problem/ etc.).

   2. Read the cluster of sentences (phrases or clauses) around the word/phrase and use context clues.

   3. Determine the part of speech of the unknown word(s).

   4. Study each word's base/prefix/suffix.

   5. Use the context of the complete passage to "guess" at the meaning.

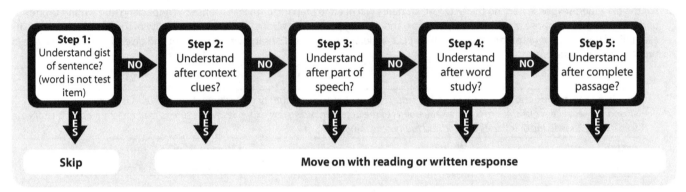

4. Have students answer the writing prompt from Strategy 2 using the information they added to the graphic organizer. A paragraph frame such as this one may guide them in this process.

The writer's argument is ___(strong/somewhat strong/somewhat weak/weak)___. The writer claims _____.

There __(is/are)__ __(1/2/3)__ strong point(s) in the argument. For instance, _____. This is a strong reason because

_____. Furthermore, the writer says _____. This is also a strong point because _____.

However, there __(is/are)__ also __(1/2/3)__ weak point(s) in the argument such as _____. This is a weak point

because _____. The writer also presents the counterargument that _____. This is a strong/weak

counterargument because _____. In conclusion, the argument is _____ since _____.

Note: Repeat Bridging Reading Strategies 1–4 for each of the two passages found in the Cumulative Review on pages 20–21 in *Writing* book 3. Student analysis of these passages will form the basis of several of the writing lessons that follow.

> ## Bridging Vocabulary

Strategy 1: *Identify the component parts and usage of new words to interpret their meanings.*

Strategy 2: *Use context clues to interpret new words, including figurative and connotative language.*

Strategy 3: *Utilize vocabulary-building resources. (Not recommended for extended response practice.)*

Strategy 4: *Build a deeper knowledge of words through writing and speaking tasks.*

1. First, present the shortest form of the word (the base word, often the verb form), followed by other commonly used word forms (if available). Examine prefixes and suffixes and their impact on word meaning and usage.

2. Read the word as used in the context of the text and discuss possible meanings given context clues and word form.

4. Gradually build a deeper knowledge of the word by having students use the word in a sentence frame, guided discussion, and an original sentence (See Appendix D, p. 144).

➤ **Bridging Written Response:** *Not Applicable*

This lesson focuses on the skills of reading and text analysis/evaluation (Trait 1 of the GED Extended-Response Scoring Rubric) and is therefore covered within the above Bridging Reading section.

➤ **Bridging Language Usage**

> **Strategy 1:** *Determine and target areas of language usage that require further development.*
>
> **Strategy 2:** *Analyze specific areas of language usage as modeled in authentic and relevant communication tasks.*
>
> **Strategy 3:** *Develop specific areas of language usage through participation in authentic communication tasks.*
>
> **Strategy 4:** *Revise language usage by utilizing peer- and self-editing checklists, rubrics, and language resources.*

1. Although minimal writing is required to synthesize the reading for this lesson, continued vigilance in monitoring ELLs' language usage is critical. Given the Bridging Reading tasks above, have students choose a language usage goal to focus on and mark it on their Language Usage Checklist (p. 129). Or, as the teacher, you may determine the language needs of the students. As an example, let's focus on the lesson Sentence Variety (p. 37) within the Check and Revise unit of the text *Writing* book 3.

2. Analyze examples from the reading or from the Bridging Reading Strategy 4 synthesis task that demonstrate the chosen language area, such as sentence variety. For example, have students in small groups scan the Guided Practice (p. 18) passage for examples of each type of sentence. Students then dissect each sentence for its dependent clauses, phrases, subjects, verbs, and conjunctions. Finally, students can write their examples and dissections on the board so that the class can check them together.

Simple Sentence	Compound Sentence	Complex Sentence
Green buildings save money as well as energy.	There is a solution (to this energy problem), however, (and) that is (to construct more "green" buildings).	Our best choice is (to conserve energy) while we develop alternative sources.

Provide a "just-in-time" mini-lesson using the Sentence Variety lesson to give students more practice with analyzing this language area.

3. To reinforce development of the language usage area, return to the Bridging Reading Strategy 4 synthesis task (the whole) and have students target this area in their writing and editing. For example, there are a number of complex sentences in the paragraph frame. Students should pay attention to these and utilize their knowledge of dependent clauses to complete these sentences correctly.

4. After the writing is complete, students can self and/or peer edit using the Editing Rubric (p. 131). Once this language goal is mastered, they can write the date of mastery on their Language Usage Checklist. Otherwise, they can revisit the goal during the next writing task.

➤ **Assessment & Next Steps**

Students should complete the suggested practice activities and the activities included in each lesson. Evaluate which learning goals were not met and remediate by using other resources, such as those identified in the Bridging Knowledge section. Upon successful completion, continue to the Cumulative Review and repeat the Bridging Reading Strategies 1–4 with these passages.

Plan and Write

CHARACTERISTICS OF GOOD RESPONSES

Skills-Based Questions

1. What are the characteristics of a good extended response on the GED test?

2. How do you make sure to include all the characteristics of a good extended response?

	Learning Goals:	**GED**
Knowledge Goals:	1. Identify the characteristics of a good extended response on the GED test.	
Reading Goals:	1. Analyze an example of an extended response to identify the characteristics that make it a good response.	
Vocabulary Goals:	1. Define test-taking vocabulary needed to prepare for the extended response item on the GED test.	R.4.1
	2. Determine the meaning of unknown vocabulary using context clues, word forms, and parts of speech.	
	3. Produce writing and speech using new vocabulary.	
Written Response Goals:	1. Summarize the extended response example and describe how it is a good example of an extended response.	W.1 W.3
	2. Use standard English language conventions. *(See Language Usage Goals)*	
Language Usage Goals:	1. Identify and correct errors in capitalization.	L.2.1
	2. Identify and correct improper sentence structure with correct punctuation.	L.2.2

Sample Instructional Support Strategies

➢ **Bridging Knowledge**

> **Strategy 1:** *Develop prior knowledge and skills to connect to new knowledge.*
>
> **Strategy 2:** *Use guiding questions to make connections beyond the lesson to broader life themes and topics.*
>
> **Strategy 3:** *Use reading strategies to develop, monitor, and synthesize new knowledge.* (See Bridging Reading)

1. Evaluate students' knowledge of the following language arts concepts and skills. Utilize the chart below to develop student background knowledge and skills as necessary.

Characteristics of Good Responses	Reading Good Responses	Writing Good Responses	Language Usage Capitalization; Commas
Writing for the GED Test Book 1: Grammar, Usage, and Mechanics			Capitalization (p. 64); Commas (p. 66)
Core Skills in Reading & Writing	Types of Essays (p. 125)	Unit 5, Lesson 1: Topic Sentences (p. 115); Lesson 2: Supporting Details (p. 118); Lesson 3: Transitions (p. 121)	Capitalization (p. 102); Commas (p. 92)
Scoreboost: Writing Across the Tests Sentence Structure, Usage, and Mechanics (SS); Responding to Text (RT)	RT: Analyze Arguments in Text (p. 4)		SS: Capitalize Correctly (p. 30); Use Commas Correctly (p. 32); Capitalization, Punctuation, and Spelling Unit Practice (p. 36)
Scoreboost: Thinking Skills Critical Thinking	Differentiate Facts from Opinion and Speculation (p. 30); Evaluate Relevance and Sufficiency of Information (p. 32)		
Pre-HSE Workbook Reading (R); Writing 1 (W1); Writing 2 (W2)	R: Arguments (p. 32)	W2: Arguments (p. 24)	W1: Capital Letters (p. 16)

2. Contextualize the lesson within a broader theme or topic by beginning the lesson with Guiding Questions that relate to the passage on page 25. Guiding questions that are authentic and relevant to students draw them deeper into the lesson and allow them to build deeper knowledge beyond the content of the lesson.

> **Guiding Questions:**
>
> 1. What makes the example regarding the use of LED light bulbs a sample of a strong extended response?
>
> 2. How can you apply these characteristics to your own extended response?

➤ Bridging Reading

Strategy 1: *Determine the type of text, establish reading purpose, and make predictions using text features and signal words.*

Strategy 2: *Develop text analysis using think-alouds, annotation, sentence frames, and graphic organizers.*

Strategy 3: *Overcome text analysis barriers using prior knowledge, analyzing language usage, and using resources.*

Strategy 4: *Synthesize text analysis using paraphrasing, text frames, graphic organizers, and peer discussions.*

1. The text presented on page 25 in this lesson is a model of a well-written extended response for the GED test. Simply help students identify the purpose of the text and their purpose for reading.

2. The lesson provides a graphic organizer showing the components of an extended response. Using the sample extended response on page 25, here is what a graphic organizer showing what an evaluation of two arguments, rather than one, would look like.

Claim: Winster's editorial is the better supported of the two arguments.		

⬇

Winster's argument		
LED bulbs last longer and save energy *Evidence:* U.S. Dept. statistic: 12-watt LED = same light as a traditional 60 watt and lasts 25 times longer with 75% energy savings	Long lasting bulbs mean people don't have to drive to the store as often to buy more *No evidence*	*Counterargument:* LEDs cost more *To refute:* But energy savings makes up this difference.

⬇

Clemmons' argument		
People only like LEDs because they want new "gadgets" *Evidence:* Name calling: "technology junkies"	CFLs give him a headache *Evidence:* Thinks maybe it would be the same with LEDs	High cost and quality of light are unsuitable *No evidence*

3. The lesson provides a list of characteristics to include in a well-written extended response (based on Trait 2 of the GED Extended-Response Scoring Rubric). Students can use the sample extended response to find models of each trait on the checklist and add them to a graphic organizer.

✓	Characteristics of a Good Response	Example:
	An introduction with a clearly state central claim	"Winster's editorial is the better supported of the two arguments because she backs up her claim with sound reasons and reliable evidence."
	A body made up of paragraphs that clearly support the central claim (paragraphs are relevant and in logical order)	1 paragraph for each argument Topic sentence, strong points, weak points, counterargument
	Enough evidence to develop ideas fully	Uses 3 points for each argument
	Paragraphs presented in a logical progression, or order	Start with strong argument, finish with weak argument
	Signal words or transitions, that show the relationships between ideas	"In contrast" "To support this reason" "In conclusion"
	Carefully chosen words and phrases that express ideas clearly	For example, the claim is well-stated and clear.
	An awareness of the audience and purpose (style and structure)	Formal style and has introduction, body, and conclusion appropriate for the extended response
	Conclusion restates the claim in a new way	Winster's editorial, which gives sound reasons and is supported by facts and statistics from a reliable source, is more convincing.

4. Have students summarize the characteristics of a good extended response supported by examples from the text.

An extended response must include ___(name the 3 parts of an extended response)___ . In the _____ , the writer must state _____ . For example, in the example on page 31, the claim is _____ . In the _____ of the response, the writer must present _____ and _____ . One example of this is _____ . The writer must also use _____ . The example response has _____ . Finally, the extended response must include _____ that _____ .

➢ Bridging Vocabulary

Strategy 1: *Identify the component parts and usage of new words to interpret their meanings.*
Strategy 2: *Use context clues to interpret new words, including figurative and connotative language.*
Strategy 3: *Utilize vocabulary-building resources. (Not recommended for extended response practice)*
Strategy 4: *Build a deeper knowledge of words through writing and speaking tasks.*

1. First, present the shortest form of the word (the base word, often the verb form), followed by other commonly used word forms (if available). Examine prefixes and suffixes and their impact on word meaning and usage.

2. Read the word as used in the context of the text and discuss possible meanings given context clues and word form.

4. Gradually build a deeper knowledge of the word by having students use the word in a sentence frame, guided discussion, and an original sentence (see Appendix D, p. 144).

➢ Bridging Written Response: *Not Applicable*

This lesson focuses on the skills of text analysis/evaluation and is therefore covered within the Bridging Reading section.

➢ Bridging Language Usage

Strategy 1: *Determine and target areas of language usage that require further development.*

Strategy 2: *Analyze specific areas of language usage as modeled in authentic and relevant communication tasks.*

Strategy 3: *Develop specific areas of language usage through participation in authentic communication tasks.*

Strategy 4: *Revise language usage by utilizing peer- and self-editing checklists, rubrics, and language resources.*

1. Although minimal writing is required to synthesize the reading for this lesson, continued vigilance in monitoring ELLs' language usage is critical. Given the Bridging Reading tasks above, have students choose a language usage goal to focus on and mark it on their Language Usage Checklist (p. 129). Or, as the teacher, you may determine the language needs of the students. As an example, for this lesson let's focus on Capitalization (p. 42) and Commas (p. 40) within the Check and Revise unit of *Writing* book 3.

2. Analyze examples from the reading that demonstrate the chosen language usage goal, such as capitalization and commas.

Capitalization:	Commas:
First letter in a sentence: *To support this reason…*	A list: *No example*
Acronyms: *CFL*	Beginning phrase: *In her counterarguments,*
Proper Nouns: *Alicia Winster, Jared Clemmons, U.S. Department of Energy*	Beginning dependent clause: *When we eat these foods,*
	Sequence and other Signal Words: *Clemmons concludes,*
	Between independent clauses before a conjunction: *He complains that compact fluorescent lamp (CFL) bulbs give him a headache …, although he has not tried them.*

Provide "just-in-time" mini-lessons using the Capitalization (p. 42) and Commas (p. 40) lessons to give students more practice with analyzing this language area.

3. To reinforce development of the language usage area, return to the Bridging Reading synthesis task (the whole) and have students target their language goal in their writing. The paragraph frame has several comma usage examples:

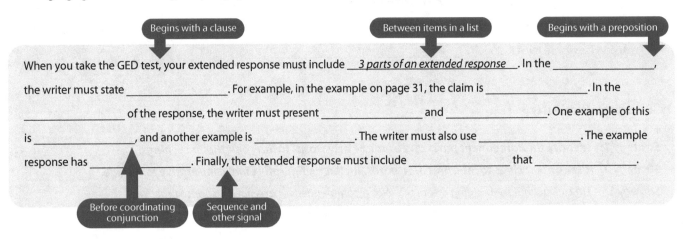

4. After the writing is complete, students can self and/or peer edit using the Editing Rubric (p. 131). Once this language goal is mastered, they can write the date of mastery on their Language Usage Checklist. Otherwise, they can revisit the goal during the next writing task.

➢ Assessment & Next Steps

Students should complete the suggested practice activities and the activities included in each lesson. Evaluate which learning goals were not met and remediate by using other resources, such as those identified in the Bridging Knowledge section. Upon successful completion, continue to the next lesson.

PLAN: DETERMINE YOUR CLAIM AND EVIDENCE

Skills-Based Questions

1. What is the central claim in your extended response?

2. What evidence will you use to support it?

	Learning Goals:	**GED**
Knowledge Goals:	1. Identify the central claim and supporting evidence in an argument.	R.8.1
		R.8.2
Reading Goals:	1. Analyze an example of an extended response to identify the claim and supporting evidence.	R.8.1
		R.8.2
Vocabulary Goals:	1. Define key subject and academic vocabulary.	R.4.1
	2. Determine the meaning of unknown vocabulary using context clues, word forms, and parts of speech.	
	3. Produce writing and speech using new vocabulary.	
Written Response Goals:	1. Determine the claim in an argument and identify evidence that supports it.	W.1
	2. State a central claim and note the evidence needed to support it.	W.2
	3. Use standard English language conventions. *(See Language Usage Goals)*	W.3
Language Usage Goals:	1. Identify and correct errors in subject-verb agreement, including complex subject-verb agreement.	L.1.2
		L.1.7

Sample Instructional Support Strategies

➢ **Bridging Knowledge**

> **Strategy 1:** *Develop prior knowledge and skills to connect to new knowledge.*
>
> **Strategy 2:** *Use guiding questions to make connections beyond the lesson to broader life themes and topics.*
>
> **Strategy 3:** *Use reading strategies to develop, monitor, and synthesize new knowledge.* (See Bridging Reading)
>
> **Strategy 4:** *Demonstrate (and further develop) synthesis of new knowledge through written student response tasks.* (See Bridging Written Response)

1. Evaluate students' knowledge of the following language arts concepts and skills. Utilize the chart below to develop student background knowledge and skills as necessary.

Plan: Determine Your Claim and Evidence	Reading Claim and Evidence	Writing Claim and Evidence	Language Usage Subject-Verb Agreement
Writing for the GED Test Book 1: Grammar, Usage, and Mechanics			Subject-Verb Agreement I (p. 48); Subject-Verb Agreement II (p. 50); Subject-Verb Agreement III (p. 52)
Core Skills in Reading & Writing	Unit 6, Lesson 1: Types of Essays (p. 125)	Unit 6, Lesson 2: Prewriting (p. 129)	Unit 4, Lesson 6: Agreement (p. 99)
Scoreboost: Writing Across the Tests Sentence Structure, Usage, and Mechanics (SS); Responding to Text (RT)	RT: Collect Supporting Details in Text (p. 7); Develop a Thesis Statement (p. 10)		SS: Make Subjects and Verbs Agree (p. 20); Make Subjects and Verbs Agree in Complicated Sentence Structures (p. 22)
Pre-HSE Workbook Reading (R); Writing 1 (W1); Writing 2 (W2)	R: Arguments (p. 32)	W2: Development of Ideas (p. 16); Relevance of Ideas (p. 18); Arguments (p. 24); Brainstorm an Argument (p. 26)	W1: Subject-Verb Agreement (p. 30)

2. The Guiding Questions for this lesson, and for the following lessons, are based on what students will be asked to address in a writing prompt. Keeping the Guiding Questions constant through these lessons will help students keep their eye on the end goal as they prepare for writing an extended response. The Guiding Questions refer to the passages in the Cumulative Review on pages 20 to 21 in *Writing* book 3.

> **Guiding Questions:**
>
> 1. Which of the two arguments—the editorial or the letter—regarding genetically modified foods is stronger?
>
> 2. What evidence from each argument supports your claim and how does this evidence support it?

➢ **Bridging Reading**

> ***Strategy 1:*** ***Determine the text type, establish reading purpose, and make predictions using text features and signal words.***
>
> ***Strategy 2:*** ***Develop text analysis using think-alouds, annotation, sentence frames, and graphic organizers.***
>
> *Strategy 3:* *Overcome text analysis barriers using prior knowledge, analyzing language usage, and using resources.*
>
> *Strategy 4:* *Synthesize text analysis using paraphrasing, text frames, graphic organizers, and peer discussions.*

1. For this lesson, students are required to review their analysis of the two passages from the Cumulative Review (pages 20 to 21 of *Writing* book 3) to determine which passage they will claim is a stronger argument and to gather evidence they will use to support their claim. Although students will not be required to respond to the prompt at this time, it is important to remind students of what the overall purpose of their reading is. Earlier in this book (Introduction to Extended Responses, p. 72), students examined the directions from a writing prompt. Have them revisit the work they did for that practice.

Writing prompt directions: *In your response, analyze both the editorial and the letter to determine which argument is stronger. Use relevant and specific evidence from both sources to support your response. Type your response in the box. This task may take approximately 45 minutes to complete.*

Action	What?	How or Why?
Analyze	the editorial and letter	to determine which is stronger
Use	relevant and specific evidence	from both sources to support response
Type	response	in the box (45 minutes)

2. If students have not already analyzed these two passages, have them do that now following the instructions below. If they have, then have them take out their notes from that analysis and continue on to the Bridging Written Response section below.

When evaluating an argument, first analyze it for its component parts (central claim, supporting evidence, and counterarguments) and then evaluate the argument for specific, relevant, and sound reasoning and reliable evidence. The strategies in the margin of the Guided Practice provide annotation practice for students by asking them to underline these components as they identify them in the text. Filling out a graphic organizer with evaluation criteria can guide students in evaluating each component. During the GED test, students will not have access to this checklist, but they can jot what they remember on the erasable noteboard in a similar fashion.

Claim:				
	Evidence	**Evidence**	**Evidence**	**Counterargument**
Text Examples:				
• Relevant & specific?				
• Sufficient?				
• Sound logic? (No? Circle below*)				
• Reliable evidence? (No? Circle below**)				
Fallacies of Logic: 1) Jump on the Bandwagon 2) Personal Attack 3) Either/Or Thinking 4) Slippery Slope				
**Unreliable Evidence: 1) not knowledgeable source 2) biased source 3) outdated information*				

➤ Bridging Vocabulary

> **Strategy 1:** *Identify the component parts and usage of new words to interpret their meanings.*
>
> **Strategy 2:** *Use context clues to interpret new words, including figurative and connotative language.*
>
> Strategy 3: *Utilize vocabulary-building resources. (Not recommended for extended response practice.)*
>
> **Strategy 4:** *Build a deeper knowledge of words through writing and speaking tasks.*

1. First, present the shortest form of the word (the base word, often the verb form), followed by other commonly used word forms (if available). Examine prefixes and suffixes and their impact on word meaning and usage.

2. Read the word as used in the context of the text and discuss possible meanings given context clues and word form.

4. Gradually build a deeper knowledge of the word by having students use the word in a sentence frame, guided discussion, and an original sentence (see Appendix D, p. 144).

➤ Bridging Written Response

> **Strategy 1:** *Prepare for a response task by identifying its purpose, audience, signal words, structure, and style.*
>
> **Strategy 2:** *Organize text analysis for written response using a graphic organizer and/or paragraph/essay frame.*
>
> Strategy 3: *Overcome barriers to producing clear/coherent writing by using models, language analysis, and resources.*
>
> Strategy 4: *Revise writing by utilizing peer- and self-editing checklists, rubrics, and writing resources.*

1. To prepare for the response task, students need to identify the writing purpose, which for this lesson is to write a claim that states which of the two arguments from the Cumulative Review is the stronger argument and why. Students have already examined the directions in the writing prompt and should understand the writing purpose. However, it will be helpful for students to prepare their signal words and language usage goal at this point.

Signal Words	*Contrast:* unlike, differ, different from, in contrast, however, on the other hand *Support:* another important point, in fact, as a matter of fact, furthermore, also *Present Evidence:* According to the argument/writer…; The argument/writer says… *Examples:* for example, such as, including, one example is, for instance, to illustrate *Conclusion:* therefore, thus, in conclusion, as such, given, for this reason
Language Usage Goal	*Student chooses a language usage area on which to focus.*

2. Students will use the graphic organizers they completed for Bridging Reading Strategy 2 to determine their claim and gather evidence to support it. However, the purpose of those graphic organizers is to *evaluate* the arguments not to *organize* their extended response. As such, students will need a different graphic organizer, like the one below (template on p. 114), to organize the information in preparation for their extended response. Students will add to this graphic organizer as they progress through lessons that follow. Have students complete the white sections of the organizer, leaving the other areas to be filled in later.

Introduction		
Claim:		
Background Information: *to add later*		
Topic Sentence: *to add later*		

⬇

Body		
Stronger Argument:		
Topic Sentence: *to add later*		
Point:	Point:	Point:
Evidence:	Evidence:	Evidence:

⬇

Body		
Weaker Argument:		
Topic Sentence: *to add later*		
Point:	Point:	Point:
Evidence:	Evidence:	Evidence:

⬇

Conclusion		
Restate the Claim: *to add later*		
Concluding Sentence: *to add later*		

3. In the lesson Characteristics of Good Responses (p. 84), students were shown a sample graphic organizer with information from the extended response on page 25 of *Writing* book 3. Use this as a model for students as they complete their own graphic organizer for their extended response.

> ## Bridging Language Usage

> **Strategy 1:** *Determine and target areas of language usage that require further development.*
>
> **Strategy 2:** *Analyze specific areas of language usage as modeled in authentic and relevant communication tasks.*
>
> **Strategy 3:** *Develop specific areas of language usage through participation in authentic communication tasks.*
>
> **Strategy 4:** *Revise language usage by utilizing peer- and self-editing checklists, rubrics, and language resources.*

1. Although minimal writing is required for this lesson, continued vigilance monitoring ELLs' language usage is critical. Have students choose a language usage goal to focus on and mark it on their Language Usage Checklist (p. 129). Or, as the teacher, you may determine the language needs of the students. As an example, for this lesson let's focus on Subject-Verb Agreement (p. 38 within the Check and Revise unit of *Writing* book 3).

2. Analyze examples from the Bridging Written Response task that demonstrate the chosen language area, such as subject-verb agreement. In particular, students will be using third-person singular to evaluate an argument, the claim, what the writer says, etc. Make sure they identify these third-person singular subjects and match each with the correct verb form. Provide a "just-in-time" mini-lesson using the Sentence-Verb Agreement lesson (p. 38) to give students more practice with analyzing this language area.

3. At this point students have just been jotting information into the graphic organizer, and most likely are not making complete sentences. However, if they are including subjects and verbs, they can pay special attention to subject-verb agreement.

4. As students are not necessarily constructing complete sentences, they may not have any proper writing to edit. However, if they do, students can self and/or peer edit using the Editing Rubric (p. 131). Once this language goal is mastered, they can write the date of mastery on their Language Usage Checklist. Otherwise, they can revisit the goal during the next writing task.

> ## Assessment & Next Steps

Students should complete the suggested practice activities and the activities included in each lesson. Evaluate which learning goals were not met and remediate by using other resources, such as those identified in the Bridging Knowledge section. Upon successful completion, continue to the next lesson.

PLAN: ORGANIZE YOUR RESPONSE

Skills-Based Questions

1. What are the characteristics of a well-organized extended response?

2. How do you make sure to include all the parts you need in your extended response?

	Learning Goals:	**GED**
Knowledge Goals:	1. Identify the characteristics of a well-organized extended response on the GED test.	
Reading Goals:	1. Analyze an example of an extended response to identify the characteristics that make it well-organized.	R.5.2
	2. Describe how parts of the text (words, phrases, clauses, and paragraphs) relate to other parts of the text.	
Vocabulary Goals:	1. Define key subject and academic vocabulary.	R.4.1
	2. Determine the meaning of unknown vocabulary using context clues, word forms, and parts of speech.	
	3. Produce writing and speech using new vocabulary.	
Written Response Goals:	1. Organize an extended response clearly and logically.	W.2
	2. Use standard English language conventions. *(See Language Usage Goals)*	W.3
Language Usage Goals:	1. Identify and correct errors in pronoun usage, including complex pronoun usage.	L.1.3
		L.1.7

Sample Instructional Support Strategies

➤ **Bridging Knowledge**

> **Strategy 1:** *Develop prior knowledge and skills to connect to new knowledge.*
>
> **Strategy 2:** *Use guiding questions to make connections beyond the lesson to broader life themes and topics.*
>
> Strategy 3: *Use reading strategies to develop, monitor, and synthesize new knowledge.*
>
> **Strategy 4:** *Demonstrate (and further develop) synthesis of new knowledge through written student response tasks.*
> *(See Bridging Written Response)*

1. Evaluate students' knowledge of the following language arts concepts and skills. Utilize the chart below to develop student background knowledge and skills as necessary.

Plan: Organize Your Response	Reading Organize Your Response	Writing Organize Your Response	Language Usage Pronoun Usage
Writing for the GED Test Book 1: Grammar, Usage, and Mechanics			Nouns and Personal Pronouns (p. 38); Other Kinds of Pronouns (p. 40); Pronoun-Antecedent Agreement (p. 54); Clear Antecedents (p. 56)
Core Skills in Reading & Writing	Unit 6, Lesson 2: Prewriting (p. 129)	Unit 6, Lesson 3: Writing the Rough Draft (p. 132)	Unit 4, Lesson 1: Parts of Speech (p. 80); Lesson 6: Agreement (p. 99)
Scoreboost: Writing Across the Tests Sentence Structure, Usage, and Mechanics (SS); Responding to Text (RT)			SS: Correct Errors in Pronoun Usage (p. 24); Fix Pronoun Agreement Problems (p. 26)
Pre-HSE Workbook Reading (R); Writing 1 (W1); Writing 2 (W2)	R: Arguments (p. 32)	W2: Organize an Argument (p. 28) Organize and Write (p. 40)	W1: Pronouns (p. 18); Pronoun Agreement (p. 22)

2. The Guiding Questions for this lesson, and for the following lessons, are based on what students will be asked to address in a writing prompt. Keeping the Guiding Questions constant through these lessons will help students keep their eye on the end goal as they prepare for writing an extended response. The Guiding Questions refer to the passages in the Cumulative Review on pages 20 to 21 in *Writing* book 3.

> **Guiding Questions:**
>
> 1. Which of the two arguments—the editorial or the letter—regarding genetically modified foods is stronger?
>
> 2. What evidence from each argument supports your claim?

➤ **Bridging Reading:** *Not Applicable*

The reading analysis that provides the basis for this lesson's written response has already been completed in earlier lessons (either in Plan: Determine Your Claim and Evidence, or as part of the Cumulative Review that followed the Evaluating Reasoning lesson).

➢ Bridging Vocabulary

Strategy 1: *Identify the component parts and usage of new words to interpret their meanings.*
Strategy 2: *Use context clues to interpret new words, including figurative and connotative language.*
Strategy 3: *Utilize vocabulary-building resources. (Not recommended for extended response practice)*
Strategy 4: *Build a deeper knowledge of words through writing and speaking tasks.*

1. First, present the shortest form of the word (the base word, often the verb form), followed by other commonly used word forms (if available). Examine prefixes and suffixes and their impact on word meaning and usage.

2. Read the word as used in the context of the text and discuss possible meanings given context clues and word form.

4. Gradually build deeper knowledge of the word by having students use the word in a sentence frame, guided discussion, and an original sentence (see Appendix D, p. 144).

➢ Bridging Written Response:

Strategy 1: *Prepare for a response task by identifying its purpose, audience, signal words, structure, and style.*
Strategy 2: *Organize text analysis for written response using a graphic organizer and/or paragraph/essay frame.*
Strategy 3: *Overcome barriers to producing clear/coherent writing by using models, language analysis, and resources.*
Strategy 4: *Revise writing by utilizing peer- and self-editing checklists, rubrics, and writing resources.*

2. Students will add to the graphic organizer (white area) they began in the previous lesson to continue organizing their writing.

Introduction		
Claim: *completed previously*		
Background Information: *to add later*		
Topic Sentence: *to add later*		

⬇

Body		
Stronger Argument: *completed previously*		
Topic Sentence: *to add later*		
Point: *completed previously*	Point: *completed previously*	Point: *completed previously*
Evidence: *completed previously*	Evidence: *completed previously*	Evidence: *completed previously*

⬇

Body		
Weaker Argument: *completed previously*		
Topic Sentence: *to add later*		
Point: *completed previously*	Point: *completed previously*	Point: *completed previously*
Evidence: *completed previously*	Evidence: *completed previously*	Evidence: *completed previously*

⬇

Conclusion	
Restate the Claim:	
Concluding Sentence: *to add later*	

3. In the lesson Characteristics of Good Responses (p. 84), students were shown a sample graphic organizer with information from the extended response on page 25 of *Writing* book 3. Have students add information to the introduction of that graphic organizer example, and have them add a conclusion. Students can use this as a model to complete the above graphic organizer for their extended response.

➤ Bridging Language Usage

> *Strategy 1:* **Determine and target areas of language usage that require further development.**
>
> *Strategy 2:* **Analyze specific areas of language usage as modeled in authentic and relevant communication tasks.**
>
> *Strategy 3:* **Develop specific areas of language usage through participation in authentic communication tasks.**
>
> *Strategy 4:* **Revise language usage by utilizing peer- and self-editing checklists, rubrics, and language resources.**

1. Although minimal writing is required for this lesson, continued vigilance monitoring ELLs' language usage is critical. Have students choose a language usage goal to focus on and mark it on their Language Usage Checklist (p. 129). Or, as the teacher, you may determine the language needs of the students. As an example, for this lesson let's focus on Pronoun Form and Agreement (p. 39 within the Check and Revise unit of *Writing* book 3).

2. Analyze examples from the reading or from the synthesis task that demonstrate the chosen language area, such as proper pronoun form and agreement. This lesson features minimal student writing to pull from, however, students can prepare for when they write their extended response. First, students should use their subject-verb agreement awareness and apply it to pronoun/verb and pronoun/antecedent agreement. Next, explain that they may need to use the possessive form such as "his claim" or "her argument" or, if the gender of the writer is unknown, "his or her claim." Likewise, students will need to use relative pronouns such as "this means" or "that shows." Finally, provide a "just-in-time" mini-lesson using the Pronoun Form and Agreement lesson (p. 39) to give students more practice with analyzing this language area.

3. At this point students have just been jotting information into the graphic organizer, and most likely are not making complete sentences. However, if they are including pronouns, they can pay special attention to pronoun form and agreement.

4. As students are not necessarily constructing complete sentences, they may not have any proper writing to edit. However, if they do, students can self and/or peer edit using the Editing Rubric (p. 131). Once this language goal is mastered, they can write the date of mastery on their Language Usage Checklist. Otherwise, they can revisit the goal during the next writing task.

➤ Assessment & Next Steps

Students should complete the suggested practice activities and the activities included in each lesson. Evaluate which learning goals were not met and remediate by using other resources, such as those identified in the Bridging Knowledge section. Upon successful completion, continue to the next lesson.

PLAN: CREATE A PROGRESSION OF IDEAS

Skills-Based Questions

1. How do you organize your ideas to best support your argument?
2. How do you organize the ideas within a paragraph?

	Learning Goals:	GED
Knowledge Goals:	1. Identify ways to organize ideas to best support an argument.	R.8.1
	2. Recognize the characteristics of a well-written paragraph.	R.5.2
Reading Goals:	1. Describe how the order of ideas supports or does not support a claim.	R.8.1
	2. Describe how parts of a paragraph go together to make a well-written paragraph.	R.5.2
Vocabulary Goals:	1. Define key subject and academic vocabulary.	R.4.1
	2. Determine the meaning of unknown vocabulary using context clues, word forms, and parts of speech.	
	3. Produce writing and speech using new vocabulary.	
Written Response Goals:	1. Organize ideas clearly and logically within in a well-written paragraph.	W.2
	2. Use standard English language conventions. *(See Language Usage Goals)*	W.3
Language Usage Goals:	1. Edit to include correct use of apostrophes.	L.2.3
	2. Identify and correct errors involving commonly confused words.	L.1.1

Sample Instructional Support Strategies

➢ Bridging Knowledge

> **Strategy 1:** *Develop prior knowledge and skills to connect to new knowledge.*
>
> **Strategy 2:** *Use guiding questions to make connections beyond the lesson to broader life themes and topics.*
>
> Strategy 3: *Use reading strategies to develop, monitor, and synthesize new knowledge.*
>
> **Strategy 4:** *Demonstrate (and further develop) synthesis of new knowledge through written student response tasks.* *(See Bridging Written Response)*

1. Evaluate students' knowledge of the following language arts concepts and skills. Utilize the chart below to develop student background knowledge and skills as necessary.

Plan: Create a Progression of Ideas	Reading Progression of Ideas	Writing Progression of Ideas	Language Usage Apostrophes and Homophones
Writing for the GED Test Book 1: Grammar, Usage, and Mechanics			Plurals and Possessives (p. 70); Words That Sound Alike (p. 72)
Core Skills in Reading & Writing	Unit 6, Lesson 2: Prewriting (p. 129)	Unit 5, Lesson 1: Topic Sentences (p. 115); Lesson 2: Supporting Details (p. 118); Lesson 3: Transitions (p. 121)	Unit 4, Lesson 5: Punctuation (p. 95); Lesson 9: Spelling (p. 108)
Scoreboost: Writing Across the Tests Sentence Structure, Usage, and Mechanics (SS); Responding to Text (RT)		RT: Organize Supporting Ideas (p. 12)	SS: Spell Well (p. 34); Capitalization, Punctuation, and Spelling unit practice (p.36)
Pre-HSE Workbook Reading (R); Writing 1 (W1); Writing 2 (W2)		W2: Paragraph structure, (pp. 12–15); Paragraph support (pp. 16–23)	W1: Nouns and Plurals (p. 14); Possessives (p. 20); Spelling (p. 32)

2. The Guiding Questions for this lesson, and for the following lessons, are based on what students will be asked to address in a writing prompt. Keeping the Guiding Questions constant through these lessons will help students keep their eye on the end goal as they prepare for writing an extended response. The Guiding Questions refer to the passages in the Cumulative Review on pages 20 to 21 in *Writing* book 3.

> **Guiding Questions:**
>
> 1. Which of the two arguments—the editorial or the letter—regarding genetically modified foods is stronger?
>
> 2. What evidence from each argument supports your claim and how does this evidence support it?

> ➤ **Bridging Reading:** *Not Applicable*

The reading analysis that provides the basis for this lesson's written response has already been completed in earlier lessons (either in Plan: Determine Your Claim and Evidence, or as part of the Cumulative Review that followed the Evaluating Reasoning lesson).

> ➤ **Bridging Vocabulary**

> *Strategy 1:* ***Identify the component parts and usage of new words to interpret their meanings.***
>
> *Strategy 2:* ***Use context clues to interpret new words, including figurative and connotative language.***
>
> *Strategy 3:* *Utilize vocabulary-building resources. (Not recommended for extended response practice.)*
>
> *Strategy 4:* ***Build a deeper knowledge of words through writing and speaking tasks.***

1. First, present the shortest form of the word (the base word, often the verb form), followed by other commonly used word forms (if available). Examine prefixes and suffixes and their impact on word meaning and usage.

2. Read the word as used in the context of the text and discuss possible meanings given context clues and word form.

4. Gradually build a deeper knowledge of the word by having students use the word in a sentence frame, guided discussion, and an original sentence (see Appendix D, p. 144).

➤ **Bridging Written Response:**

Strategy 1: *Prepare for a response task by identifying its purpose, audience, signal words, structure, and style.*

Strategy 2: Organize text analysis for written response using a graphic organizer and/or paragraph/essay frame.

Strategy 3: Overcome barriers to producing clear/coherent writing by using models, language analysis, and resources.

Strategy 4: *Revise writing by utilizing peer- and self-editing checklists, rubrics, and writing resources.*

2. Using the graphic organizer students worked on in the previous Bridging lesson, students will add a topic sentence for each paragraph and a concluding sentence at the end (gray areas). They will then check the order of their ideas to determine if it is logical and if it follows one of the suggested patterns from the lesson.

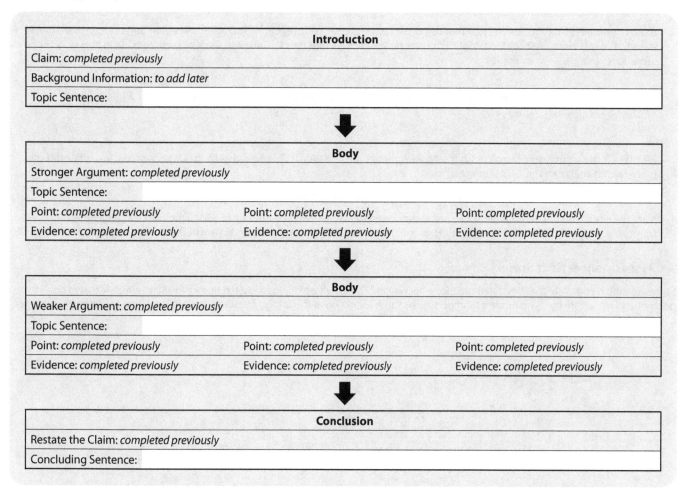

3. Continue to refer to the extended response example from the lesson Characteristics of Good Responses that goes with the sample extended response in *Writing* book 3 (p. 25). Have students examine the topic sentences for each paragraph and the progression of ideas that follow as an example. Students can check their own work against that model and make adjustments to their own work accordingly.

➤ Bridging Language Usage

> **Strategy 1:** *Determine and target areas of language usage that require further development.*
>
> **Strategy 2:** *Analyze specific areas of language usage as modeled in authentic and relevant communication tasks.*
>
> **Strategy 3:** *Develop specific areas of language usage through participation in authentic communication tasks.*
>
> **Strategy 4:** *Revise language usage by utilizing peer- and self-editing checklists, rubrics, and language resources.*

1. Although minimal writing is required for this lesson, continued vigilance monitoring ELLs' language usage is critical. Have students choose a language usage goal to focus on and mark it on their Language Usage Checklist (p. 129). Or, as the teacher, you may determine the language needs of the students. As an example, for this lesson let's focus Apostrophes and Words That Sound Alike (p. 41 and p. 43 within the Check and Revise unit of *Writing* book 3).

2. Analyze examples from the writing task that demonstrate the chosen language area, such as apostrophes and homophones. In this lesson, students write topic sentences for each paragraph. It is likely that they will need to use a possessive noun in at least one of these sentences. Here are a few examples:

   > The *writer's* argument; The letter *writer's* claim; the *argument's* main point; One of the *writer's* reasons; The *editorial's* evidence; The *letter's* greatest strength; etc.

   Provide a "just-in-time" mini-lesson using the Apostrophes (p. 41) and Words That Sound Alike (p. 43) lessons to give students more practice with analyzing this language area.

3. Have students target this language area as they write their topic sentences.

4. After the writing is complete, students can self and/or peer edit using the Editing Rubric (p. 131). Once this language goal is mastered, they can write the date of mastery on their Language Usage Checklist. Otherwise, they can revisit the goal during the next writing task.

➤ Assessment & Next Steps

Students should complete the suggested practice activities and the activities included in each lesson. Evaluate which learning goals were not met and remediate by using other resources, such as those identified in the Bridging Knowledge section. Upon successful completion, continue to next lesson.

WRITE A RESPONSE / EVALUATE YOUR RESPONSE

Skills-Based Questions

1. Which argument is stronger and why?
2. How do you support and organize your argument?
3. How do you evaluate your own argument to determine if it is strong?

	Learning Goals:	**GED**
Knowledge Goals:	1. Identify the criteria for writing a strong extended response.	R.8.1
	2. Identify a central claim and supporting evidence in an argument.	R.8.2
	3. Determine the strength of an argument based on its support and organization.	R.8.3
		R.8.5
Reading Goals:	1. Determine the author's claim, the points in his/her argument, and how they build on one another to support the claim.	R.8.1
		R.8.2
	2. Identify evidence the author uses to support a claim or conclusion.	R.8.3
	3. Evaluate how well the author supports his or her claim.	R.8.4
	4. Determine which claims are supported by evidence and which are not.	R.8.5
	5. Determine if the reasoning in an argument is valid and how false reasoning affects the argument.	R.9.3
	6. Compare and contrast how two texts on the same topic support their arguments.	
Vocabulary Goals:	1. Define key subject and academic vocabulary.	R.4.1
	2. Determine the meaning of unknown vocabulary using context clues, word forms, and parts of speech.	
	3. Produce writing and speech using new vocabulary.	
Written Response Goals:	1. Determine what is stated in the text and make valid claims supported by text evidence.	W.1
	2. Respond to text by introducing claims clearly, organizing information logically, supporting claims with text evidence, and keeping focus on the claim at hand.	W.2
		W.3
	3. Use standard English language conventions. *(See Language Usage Goals)*	
Language Usage Goals:	1. Use standard English grammar, punctuation, and mechanics.	W.3

Sample Instructional Support Strategies

➤ Bridging Knowledge

> *Strategy 1:* **Develop prior knowledge and skills to connect to new knowledge.**
>
> *Strategy 2:* **Use guiding questions to make connections beyond the lesson to broader life themes and topics.**
>
> *Strategy 3:* Use reading strategies to develop, monitor, and synthesize new knowledge.
>
> *Strategy 4:* **Demonstrate (and further develop) synthesis of new knowledge through written student response tasks.**
> (See Bridging Written Response)

1. For this lesson, students are synthesizing everything they learned about preparing for and writing a good extended response. If students still have gaps in particular areas, return to the previous lessons to provide extra practice.

2. The Guiding Questions for this lesson, and for the previous three lessons, are based on what students will be asked to address in a writing prompt. Keeping the Guiding Questions constant through these lessons will help students keep their eye on the end goal. The Guiding Questions refer to the passages in the Cumulative Review on pages 20 to 21 in *Writing* book 3.

> **Guiding Questions:**
>
> 1. Which of the two arguments—the editorial or the letter—regarding genetically modified foods is stronger?
>
> 2. What evidence from each argument supports your claim and how does this evidence support it?

➤ Bridging Reading Bridging Reading: *Not Applicable*

The reading analysis that provides the basis for this lesson's written response has already been completed in earlier lessons (either in Plan: Determine Your Claim and Evidence, or as part of the Cumulative Review that followed the Evaluating Reasoning lesson).

➤ Bridging Vocabulary

> *Strategy 1:* **Identify the component parts and usage of new words to interpret their meanings.**
>
> *Strategy 2:* **Use context clues to interpret new words, including figurative and connotative language.**
>
> *Strategy 3:* Utilize vocabulary-building resources. (Not recommended for extended response practice.)
>
> *Strategy 4:* **Build a deeper knowledge of words through writing and speaking tasks.**

1. First, present the shortest form of the word (the base word, often the verb form), followed by other commonly used word forms (if available). Examine prefixes and suffixes and their impact on word meaning and usage.

2. Read the word as used in the context of the text and discuss possible meanings given context clues and word form.

4. Gradually build a deeper knowledge of the word by having students use the word in a sentence frame, guided discussion, and an original sentence (See Appendix D, p. 144).

➢ Bridging Written Response

Strategies 1–3 have been used consistently in the previous lessons to prepare students for the extended response. The following is a reminder of each strategy used in the past few lessons.

> **Strategy 1:** *Prepare for a response task by identifying its purpose, audience, signal words, structure, and style.*
>
> **Strategy 2:** *Organize text analysis for written response using a graphic organizer and/or paragraph/essay frame.*
>
> **Strategy 3:** *Overcome barriers to producing clear/coherent writing by using models, language analysis, and resources.*
>
> **Strategy 4:** *Revise writing by utilizing peer and self editing checklists and rubrics and writing resources.*

1. Students identified the writing purpose by "unpacking" the directions in the writing prompt found on page 32 of *Writing* book 3.

Writing prompt directions: *In your response, analyze both the editorial and the letter to determine which argument is stronger. Use relevant and specific evidence from both sources to support your response. Type your response in the box. This task may take approximately 45 minutes to complete.*

Action	What?	How or Why?
Analyze	the editorial and letter	to determine which is stronger
Use	relevant and specific evidence	from both sources to support response
Type	response	in the box (45 minutes)

Then, they prepared signal words to match their written response to the purpose.

Signal Words	
	Contrast: unlike, differ, different from, in contrast, however, on the other hand
	Support: another important point, in fact, as a matter of fact, furthermore, also
	Present Evidence: According to the argument/writer…; The argument/writer says…
	Examples: for example, such as, including, one example is, for instance, to illustrate
	Conclusion: therefore, thus, in conclusion, as such, given, for this reason

2. Students used two kinds of graphic organizers to prepare for the writing task. The first helped them evaluate each of the arguments.

Argument 1:				
Claim:				
	Evidence	**Evidence**	**Evidence**	**Counterargument**
Text Examples:				
• Relevant & specific?				
• Sufficient?				
• Sound logic? (No? Circle below*)				
• Reliable evidence? (No? Circle below**)				
*Fallacies of Logic: 1) Jump on the Bandwagon 2) Personal Attack 3) Either/Or Thinking 4) Slippery Slope				
**Unreliable Evidence: 1) not knowledgeable source 2) biased source 3) outdated information				

The second helped them organize their own written response.

Introduction
Claim:
Background Information:
Topic Sentence:

↓

Body		
Stronger Argument:		
Topic Sentence:		
Point:	Point:	Point:
Evidence:	Evidence:	Evidence:

↓

Body		
Weaker Argument:		
Topic Sentence:		
Point:	Point:	Point:
Evidence:	Evidence:	Evidence:

↓

Conclusion
Restate the Claim:
Concluding Sentence:

3. Now students must put all their preparation to use by writing an extended response. They will not be able to use resources to aid them during the actual test but for this practice, they should use their graphic organizers. Students may also use, on a limited basis, vocabulary and grammar resources. They should not rely too heavily on these as they are trying to build their capacity to utilize what they already know rather than add knowledge to what they know.

4. Following the Write a Response lesson in *Writing* book 3 is the lesson Evaluate Your Response. This lesson includes a checklist to evaluate the student's evaluation of the arguments (Trait 1 of the GED scoring rubric) and to evaluate the student's development of ideas and organizational structure (Trait 2 of the GED scoring rubric). *Bridging* offers an alternative to this checklist, providing an Extended-Response Evaluation Rubric (p. 132) that provides more specific direction for the "editor" and allows a "score" for each component. The use of either the checklist or the rubric are helpful for students to develop awareness of what makes a good extended response, identify weaknesses in their writing, and revise their response accordingly.

➤ Bridging Language Usage

> **Strategy 1:** **Determine and target areas of language usage that require further development.**
>
> *Strategy 2:* *Analyze specific areas of language usage as modeled in authentic and relevant communication tasks.*
>
> **Strategy 3:** **Develop specific areas of language usage through participation in authentic communication tasks.**
>
> **Strategy 4:** **Revise language usage by utilizing peer- and self-editing checklists, rubrics, and language resources.**

1. Students should continue to work on the target areas of language usage as noted on their Language Usage Checklist (p. 129).

3. The extended response practice is about as close as you can get to the real GED, therefore students are receiving highly authentic practice using their language usage knowledge and skills. At this point, it is important that they do as much as they can from memory, however, referring to a grammar resource from time to time should be fine.

4. After the writing is complete, students will have ample opportunities to self and peer edit their work using editing checklists and rubrics and language resources.

➤ Assessment & Next Steps

Students should complete the suggested practice activities and the activities included in each lesson. Evaluate which learning goals were not met and remediate by using other resources, such as those identified in the Bridging Knowledge section. Upon successful completion, continue to the Check and Revise lessons.

Check and Revise

Skills-Based Questions

1. How do you write using standard English language conventions such as sentence structure, grammar, and mechanics?

2. How do you revise your writing to correct errors in sentence structure, grammar, and mechanics?

	Learning Goals:	GED
Knowledge Goals:	1. Identify proper use of sentence structure, grammar, and mechanics.	
Reading Goals:	1. Determine how parts of the text (words, phrases, clauses, and paragraphs) fit into the structure and message of the complete text.	R.5.1
		R.5.2
	2. Describe how parts of the text (words, phrases, clauses, and paragraphs) relate to other parts of the text.	R.5.3
	3. Identify signal words that show relationships in the text and determine how they affect the meaning and/or purpose of the text.	R.5.4
	4. Determine how a section of the text affects meaning or supports the author's purpose.	
Vocabulary Goals:	1. Determine the meaning of unknown vocabulary using word forms, and parts of speech.	R.4.1
	2. Identify and correct errors involving commonly confused words.	L.1.1
Written Response Goals:	1. Use standard English grammar, punctuation, and mechanics. *(See Language Usage Goals)*	W.3
Language Usage Goals:	1. Identify and correct errors involving commonly confused words.	L.1.1
	2. Identify and correct errors in subject-verb agreement.	L.1.2
	3. Identify and correct errors in pronoun usage.	L.1.3
	4. Identify and correct word order.	L.1.5
	5. Edit to include correct complex sentences.	L.1.6
	6. Identify and correct errors in complex subject-verb agreement and pronoun usage.	L.1.7
	7. Identify and improve unnecessary repetition and unclear sentence structure.	L.1.8
	8. Identify and correct errors in capitalization.	L.2.1
	9. Identify and correct improper sentence structure with correct punctuation.	L.2.2
	10. Edit to include correct use of apostrophes.	L.2.3
	11. Identify and correct errors in punctuation.	L.2.4

Sample Instructional Support Strategies

➢ Bridging Knowledge

See the Bridging Language Usage Cross-Reference Guide (p. 133) for a complete cross-referenced list of New Readers Press grammar resources that support GED preparation.

➢ Bridging Reading

See the Bridging lessons that support *Writing* book 2 for ways to integrate language usage areas into reading activities.

➢ Bridging Vocabulary

Familiarize students with language usage vocabulary as they practice each area. Specific vocabulary can lead to specific language usage areas that in turn lead to awareness of problem areas. This, therefore, results in correcting those problem areas and a progressive mastery of language usage.

➢ Bridging Written Response

See the Bridging lessons that support *Writing* books 2 and 3 for ways to integrate language usage areas into writing activities.

➢ Bridging Language Usage

> **Strategy 1:** *Determine and target areas of language usage that require further development.*
>
> **Strategy 2:** *Analyze specific areas of language usage as modeled in authentic and relevant communication tasks.*
>
> **Strategy 3:** *Develop specific areas of language usage through participation in authentic communication tasks.*
>
> **Strategy 4:** *Revise language usage by utilizing peer- and self-editing checklists, rubrics, and language resources.*

1–2. As mentioned in the introduction, developing language usage in its various facets (sentence structure, grammar, mechanics, etc.) is most effective when practiced within authentic communicative activities or tasks. The best way to do this is to provide "just-in-time" mini-lessons on language usage (the parts) within the main learning activities of reading, writing, and conversation (the whole). "Just-in-time" mini-lessons focus on areas of language usage students struggle with in the context of the main activity of the lesson. The Language Usage Checklist (p. 129) is a tool that can help students set and monitor their language usage goals.

If you find yourself thinking, "But my students need *everything* just-in-time!" you are not alone. In fact, if this is true for your students, you are at an advantage. Given groups of students with similar language needs, you can plan ahead and determine which language usage areas to integrate into which tasks. If this is not the case, responding to students' needs and language goals day-to-day may be your most effective option.

3. *Bridging* provides contextualization of language usage practice by:

   1. Providing suggestions on responding to students' needs and goals as they are revealed during lessons and assessments

   2. Integrating the different lessons from the Check and Revise unit into the lesson plans that support *Writing* book 3's Read and Analyze and Plan and Write units

   Whichever direction you take, you are providing an effective way for your students to develop their language usage through integration.

   This book integrates the eight language usage lessons in this unit into the Read and Analyze and Plan and Write units as examples of language usage goals students might choose to address. Now that each of the lessons have been used as an example, the remainder of this book will indicate that students should "choose focus area" and refer to their Language Usage Checklist to identify the areas that need more practice. Teachers can use strategies from previous examples to address students' goals.

4. Self and peer editing are tried-and-true ways to help students become aware of their language errors, utilize strategies to revise them, and be accountable for the quality of their own writing. Bridging includes two tools to help students in this process. One is the Language Usage Checklist (p. 129) mentioned above. This provides a list of all the sentence structure, grammar and usage, and mechanics areas that are evaluated on the GED test. Students can set a language goal, follow the listed actions to practice that language usage area, and note when their language goal is met. The second tool is the Editing Rubric (p. 131). Students can use this to evaluate their own language usage or that of a peer by reviewing each of the 10 areas by following the editing actions and scoring the level of mastery.

Timed Extended-Response Practice

PRACTICE THE RLA EXTENDED RESPONSE

Skills-Based Questions

1. Which argument is stronger and why?
2. How do you support and organize your argument?
3. How do you write an extended response that has all the necessary components?
4. How do you evaluate your own argument to determine if it is strong?

	Learning Goals:	**GED**
Knowledge Goals:	1. Identify the criteria for writing a strong extended response.	R.8.1
	2. Identify a central claim and supporting evidence in an argument.	R.8.2
	3. Determine the strength of an argument based on its support and organization.	R.8.3
		R.8.5
Reading Goals:	1. Determine the author's claim, the points in his/her argument, and how they build on one another to support the claim.	R.8.1
		R.8.2
	2. Identify evidence the author uses to support a claim or conclusion.	R.8.3
	3. Evaluate how well the author supports his or her claim.	R.8.4
	4. Determine which claims are supported by evidence and which are not.	R.8.5
	5. Determine if the reasoning in an argument is valid and how false reasoning affects the argument.	R.9.3
	6. Compare and contrast how two texts on the same topic support their arguments.	
Vocabulary Goals:	1. Define key subject and academic vocabulary.	R.4.1
	2. Determine the meaning of unknown vocabulary using context clues, word forms, and parts of speech.	
	3. Produce writing and speech using new vocabulary.	
Written Response Goals:	1. Determine what is stated in the text and make valid claims supported by text evidence.	W.1
	2. Respond to text by introducing claims clearly, organizing information logically, supporting claims with text evidence, and keeping focus on the claim at hand.	W.2
		W.3
	3. Use standard English language conventions. *(See Language Usage Goals)*	
Language Usage Goals:	1. Use standard English grammar, punctuation, and mechanics.	W.3

Sample Instructional Support Strategies

> ## Bridging Knowledge

Strategy 1: *Develop prior knowledge and skills to connect to new knowledge.*

Strategy 2: *Use guiding questions to make connections beyond the lesson to broader life themes and topics.*

Strategy 3: *Use reading strategies to develop, monitor, and synthesize new knowledge.* (See Bridging Reading)

Strategy 4: *Demonstrate (and further develop) synthesis of new knowledge through written student response tasks.* (See Bridging Written Response)

1. For this lesson, students are synthesizing everything they learned about preparing for and writing a good extended response. If students still have gaps in particular areas, return to the previous lessons to provide them with extra practice.

2. The Guiding Questions for this lesson took the directions in the writing prompt on page 46 of *Writing* book 3 and phrased them in the form of questions. This questions helps students keep their eye on the end goal of the extended response.

> ### Guiding Questions:
>
> 1. Which of the two arguments—the speech or the letter—regarding water conservation is stronger?
>
> 2. What evidence from each argument supports your claim and how does this evidence support it?

> ## Bridging Reading

Strategy 1: *Determine the type of text, establish reading purpose, and make predictions using text features and signal words.*

Strategy 2: *Develop text analysis using think-alouds, annotation, sentence frames, and graphic organizers.*

Strategy 3: *Overcome text analysis barriers using prior knowledge, analyzing language usage, and using resources.*

Strategy 4: *Synthesize text analysis using paraphrasing, text frames, graphic organizers, and peer discussions.*

1. For the extended-response item on the GED test, students will need to prepare for their response by "unpacking" the writing prompt and understanding the purpose of the reading passages. Here is the writing prompt for this lesson.

Description: *Both the speech and the letter to the editor support water conservation, but the speech encourages individual water conservation efforts, while the letter to the editor argues that it is more important for industries to conserve water.*		
Directions: *In your response, analyze both the speech and the letter to determine which position has the stronger arguments. Use relevant and specific evidence from both sources to support your response.*		
Action	**What?**	**How or Why?**
Text Purpose:		

2. Evaluating an argument consists of first analyzing it for its component parts (central claim, supporting evidence, and counterarguments) and then evaluating the argument for specific, relevant, and sound reasoning and reliable evidence. Filling out a graphic organizer (for each argument) with evaluation criteria can guide students in evaluating each component. During the actual GED test, students will not have access to this checklist, but they can jot what they remember on the erasable noteboard in a similar fashion.

Argument 1:				
Claim:				
	Evidence	**Evidence**	**Evidence**	**Counterargument**
Text Examples:				
• Relevant & specific?				
• Sufficient?				
• Sound logic? (No? Circle below*)				
• Reliable evidence? (No? Circle below**)				
Fallacies of Logic: 1) Jump on the Bandwagon 2) Personal Attack 3) Either/Or Thinking 4) Slippery Slope				
**Unreliable Evidence: 1) not knowledgeable source 2) biased source 3) outdated information*				

3. Since ELLs will not be able to use resources to help them understand the passages on the GED test, it is best if they do not use Strategy 3 when they practice for the extended response. Instead, after they identify language they do not understand in the passage, have them use a five-step process to figure out confusing areas (see flowchart below):

1. Read the sentence for gist: who, where, when, what (are they doing/is happening/is the problem/ etc.).

2. Read the cluster of sentences (phrases or clauses) around the word/phrase and use context clues.

3. Determine the part of speech of the unknown word(s).

4. Study each word's base/prefix/suffix.

5. Use the context of the complete passage to "guess" at the meaning.

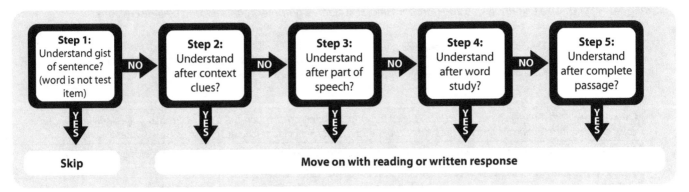

➤ Bridging Vocabulary

> **Strategy 1:** *Identify the component parts and usage of new words to interpret their meanings.*
>
> **Strategy 2:** *Use context clues to interpret new words, including figurative and connotative language.*
>
> Strategy 3: *Utilize vocabulary-building resources. (Not recommended for extended response practice.)*
>
> **Strategy 4:** *Build a deeper knowledge of words through writing and speaking tasks.*

1. First, present the shortest form of the word (the base word, often the verb form), followed by other commonly used word forms (if available). Examine prefixes and suffixes and their impact on word meaning and usage.

2. Read the word as used in the context of the text and discuss possible meanings given context clues and word form.

4. Gradually build a deeper knowledge of the word by having students use the word in a sentence frame, guided discussion, and an original sentence (see Appendix D, p. 144).

➤ Bridging Written Response

> **Strategy 1:** *Prepare for a response task by identifying its purpose, audience, signal words, structure, and style.*
>
> **Strategy 2:** *Organize text analysis for written response using a graphic organizer and/or paragraph/essay frame.*
>
> **Strategy 3:** *Overcome barriers to producing clear/coherent writing by using models, language analysis, and resources.*
>
> **Strategy 4:** *Revise writing by utilizing peer- and self-editing checklists, rubrics, and writing resources.*

1. Students identified the writing purpose by "unpacking" the writing prompt in Bridging Reading Strategy 1. They should review the prompt and then prepare the signal words they may want to use to match their written response to the purpose. For the actual GED test, they may want to jot some of these signal words down on the erasable noteboard.

Signal Words	Contrast: *unlike, differ, different from, in contrast, however, on the other hand*
	Support: *another important point, in fact, as a matter of fact, furthermore, also*
	Present Evidence: *According to the argument/writer; The argument/writer says*
	Examples: *for example, such as, including, one example is, for instance, to illustrate*
	Conclusion: *therefore, thus, in conclusion, as such, given, for this reason*

2. Now students will organize their own argument by filling in a graphic organizer like the one they completed in previous planning lessons. Have them complete the graphic organizer using this 10-step process:

   1. Write the claim.

   2. Note the titles of the stronger and weaker arguments in the correct locations.

   3. Note at least 2 points given to support each argument.

   4. Note the evidence the writer gives for each point and any problems with the reasoning or reliability.

   5. Note the counterargument the writer offers (if there is one) and how it is refuted (if it is).

   6. Fill in the background information for the introduction.

   7. Restate the claim in the conclusion.

   8. Write a topic sentence (or sentences) for the introduction that includes the claim.

   9. Write a topic sentence for each paragraph in the body.

   10. Write a concluding sentence (or sentences) for the conclusion that restates the claim.

Introduction
Claim:
Background Information:
Topic Sentence:

⬇

Body		
Stronger Argument:		
Topic Sentence:		
Point:	Point:	Point:
Evidence:	Evidence:	Evidence:

⬇

Body		
Weaker Argument:		
Topic Sentence:		
Point:	Point:	Point:
Evidence:	Evidence:	Evidence:

⬇

Conclusion
Restate the Claim:
Concluding Sentence:

3. Now students must put their preparation to use by writing the extended response. They will not be able to use resources to aid them during the actual test but for this practice, they should use their graphic organizers. At this point, students should not use vocabulary or grammar resources to help them, as this practice should mirror the GED test as much as possible. Students should make sure to integrate the signal words they jotted down as well as what they learned in the "just-in-time" language usage mini-lessons.

4. When students complete their extended response, they should first evaluate it for how well supported, developed, and organized it is and edit it for proper language usage. Have students use the Extended-Response Evaluation Rubric (p. 132) and revise their writing based on their findings. Then students will need to use the Editing Rubric (p. 131) and edit their writing based on those findings. Neither rubric will be available when they take the GED test but extra opportunities to practice with these rubrics will allow students to better internalize the self-evaluation process.

➢ Bridging Language Usage

Strategy 1:   Determine and target areas of language usage that require further development.

Strategy 2:   Analyze specific areas of language usage as modeled in authentic and relevant communication tasks.

Strategy 3:   Develop specific areas of language usage through participation in authentic communication tasks.

Strategy 4:   Revise language usage by utilizing peer- and self-editing checklists, rubrics, and language resources.

4. As stated above, students will use the Editing Rubric (p. 131) to find their errors and edit their writing.

➢ Assessment & Next Steps

Students should complete the suggested practice activities and the activities included in each lesson. Evaluate which learning goals were not met and remediate by using other resources, such as those identified in the Bridging Knowledge section. Upon successful completion, continue to the next lesson.

Short-Answer Responses

SUMMARIZING A SCIENCE PASSAGE

Skills-Based Questions

1. What is the three-step approach to summarizing a passage?
2. What do you need to include in a well-written summary?

	Learning Goals:	**GED**
Knowledge Goals:	1. Describe the three steps of the summarizing process.	R.2.1
	2. Identify the overall main idea of a passage and the main ideas of the supporting paragraphs.	R.2.4
	3. Identify or infer the topic sentence of each.	
Reading Goals:	1. Identify and comprehend the overall main idea of a passage as well as the main ideas of the supporting passages.	R.2.1
		R.2.4
	2. Find or infer the topic sentences for each main idea.	
Vocabulary Goals:	1. Define key subject and academic vocabulary.	R.4.1
	2. Determine meaning of unknown vocabulary using context clues, word forms, and parts of speech.	
	3. Produce writing and speech using new vocabulary.	
Written Response Goals:	1. Determine the main ideas of the text and the details that support them.	W.1
	2. Respond to text by summarizing information clearly, organizing information sequentially, and focusing on the writing task.	W.2
		W.3
	3. Use standard English language conventions. *(See Language Usage Goals)*	
Language Usage Goals:	1. Use standard English grammar, punctuation, and mechanics.	W.3

Sample Instructional Support Strategies

➢ Bridging Knowledge

Strategy 1: *Develop prior knowledge and skills to connect to new knowledge.*

Strategy 2: *Use guiding questions to make connections beyond the lesson to broader life themes and topics.*

Strategy 3: *Use reading strategies to develop, monitor, and synthesize new knowledge. (See Bridging Reading)*

Strategy 4: *Demonstrate (and further develop) synthesis of new knowledge through written student response tasks. (See Bridging Written Response)*

1. Evaluate students' knowledge of the following language arts concepts and skills. Utilize the chart below to develop student background knowledge and skills as necessary.

Summarizing a Science Passage	Reading Summarizing	Writing Summary	Language Usage Choose focus area
Writing for the GED Test Book 1: Grammar, Usage, and Mechanics			*Corresponding materials will vary based on the language usage area students choose to focus on.*
Core Skills in Reading & Writing	Unit 3, Lesson 2: Main Idea and Supporting Details (p. 59); Lesson 6: Summarizing (p. 71)		
Scoreboost: Writing Across the Tests Sentence Structure, Usage, and Mechanics (SS); Responding to Text (RT)		RT: Summarize Main Idea or Theme (p. 31); Identify Specific Details in Text (p. 33)	
Scoreboost: Thinking Skills Critical Thinking	Understand Central Ideas & Supporting Information (p. 4)	Summarize Ideas (p. 6)	
Pre-HSE Workbook Reading (R); Writing 1 (W1); Writing 2 (W2)	R: Main Idea (p. 20); Supporting Details (p. 22)		

2. Contextualize the Guided Practice portion of the lesson (p. 55) within a broader theme or topic by beginning the lesson with Guiding Questions. Guiding questions that are authentic and relevant to students draw them deeper into the lesson and allow them to build deeper knowledge beyond the content of the lesson.

Guiding Questions:

1. What is the main idea of the passage *Why Pluto Was Demoted*?

2. What is the main idea of each of the supporting paragraphs?

➤ **Bridging Reading**

> **Strategy 1:** *Determine the type of text, establish reading purpose, and make predictions using text features and signal words.*
>
> **Strategy 2:** *Develop text analysis using think-alouds, annotation, sentence frames, and graphic organizers.*
>
> **Strategy 3:** *Overcome text analysis barriers using prior knowledge, analyzing language usage, and using resources.*
>
> **Strategy 4:** *Synthesize text analysis using paraphrasing, text frames, graphic organizers, and peer discussions.*

1. Students will read the test prompt (GED Practice) to determine the purpose of the reading task. Then, they should scan the text for text features and signal words to determine the type of text and its purpose.

Guided Practice:	*Why Pluto Was Demoted*
Test Prompt (GED Practice):	Use the main ideas that you found to write a three- or four- sentence summary of the passage.
Reading Purpose:	Summarize the passage in 3 to 4 sentences using the main ideas.
Text Purpose:	Informational

2. The lesson Summarizing a Science Passage provides a three-step process for students to summarize science passages on the GED test. Step 1 in this process is Read and Analyze the Passage. As part of this step, the lesson suggests that students skim the passage for the overall main idea and the main ideas in each paragraph. This is where students' past annotation strategies pay off. Students should find the topic sentence in each paragraph. If they cannot find a topic sentence, they need to ask: who, where, when, and what (is most important) to make a topic sentence.

3. Since students will not be able to use resources to help them understand the passages on the GED test, it is best if they do not use Strategy 3 when they practice for the extended response. Instead, after they identify language they do not understand in the passage, have them use a five-step process to figure out confusing areas (see flowchart below):

   1. Read the sentence for gist: who, where, when, what (are they doing/is happening/is the problem/ etc.).

   2. Read the cluster of sentences (phrases or clauses) around the word/phrase and use context clues.

   3. Determine the part of speech of the unknown word(s).

   4. Study each word's base/prefix/suffix.

   5. Use the context of the complete passage to "guess" at the meaning.

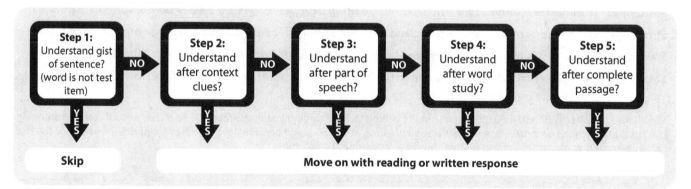

4. Students need to paraphrase each paragraph's topic sentence after they identify it. Usually, they will need to include important information not directly stated in the topic sentence.

Topic sentence, paragraph 2:

Finally, in 2003, [they made a discovery] that would lead to a more exact definition of the term *planet*.

Scientists discovered Eris and questioned whether or not it was a planet.

Eris was similar to Pluto.

Paraphrase: Scientists discovered Eris and began to question the definition of a planet. Since Pluto is similar to Eris, Pluto's status as a planet was questioned, too.

➢ Bridging Vocabulary

Strategy 1: *Identify the component parts and usage of new words to interpret their meanings.*

Strategy 2: *Use context clues to interpret new words, including figurative and connotative language.*

Strategy 3: *Utilize vocabulary-building resources.*

Strategy 4: *Build a deeper knowledge of words through writing and speaking tasks.*

1. First, present the shortest form of the word (the base word, often the verb form), followed by other commonly used word forms (if available). Examine prefixes and suffixes and their impact on word meaning and usage.

2. Read the word as used in the context of the text and discuss possible meanings given context clues and word form.

3. Have students find (electronically or in print) the definition or translation of the base form and, if different, the form used in context and note these definitions for future reference and study.

4. Gradually build a deeper knowledge of the word by having students use the word in a sentence frame, guided discussion, and an original sentence (see Appendix D, p. 144).

➢ Bridging Written Response

Strategy 1: *Prepare for a response task by identifying its purpose, audience, signal words, structure, and style.*

Strategy 2: *Organize text analysis for written response using a graphic organizer and/or paragraph/essay frame.*

Strategy 3: *Overcome barriers to producing clear/coherent writing by using models, language analysis, and resources.*

Strategy 4: *Revise writing by utilizing peer- and self-editing checklists, rubrics, and writing resources.*

Strategy 5: *Extend text analysis to build upon initial information or claims by using evidence from additional sources.*

1. Students have already determined the purpose of the writing task in Bridging Reading Strategy 1. Now they should consider some signal words that match the purpose. Since the task is to summarize, obviously summary signal words will be helpful. Similarly, since the topic is science-related, cause and effect and sequencing signal words may be helpful.

Signal Words	Summary: *in summary, to summarize, overall, to sum up, on the whole, in general*
	Cause/effect: *due to, since, in order to, because of, therefore, consequently, as a result*
	Process/sequence: *First, second, next, then, after, since, prior to, during, finally*

2. Step 2 in the three-step summary process is Plan and Write. Students need to organize their ideas in a way that fits the conventions of the writing purpose. For a summary, students should sequence their paraphrased sentences starting with the general overall main idea followed by the supporting main ideas. The supporting main ideas should follow the same sequence as the original passage. After students organize their ideas, they should be able to successfully write their summary.

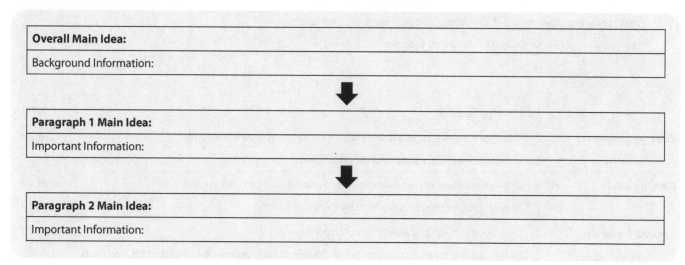

3. Continue to stress that students will need to use their knowledge of vocabulary and language usage to construct their written responses on the GED test. If they can think back to a grammar or vocabulary activity or visualize one of their vocabulary or grammar resources, it may help them retrieve information from their memory and enable them to apply it to the task at hand.

4. Have students use the checklist provided in the lesson to complete Step 3: Check and Revise.

   • Did I correctly identify and restate the overall main idea?

   • Did I restate the main idea or ideas of each paragraph?

   • Did I use my own words?

   • Does my writing sound fluent?

   • Is my writing clear?

➢ Bridging Language Usage

> *Strategy 1:* **Determine and target areas of language usage that require further development.**
>
> *Strategy 2:* *Analyze specific areas of language usage as modeled in authentic and relevant communication tasks.*
>
> *Strategy 3:* **Develop specific areas of language usage through participation in authentic communication tasks.**
>
> *Strategy 4:* **Revise language usage by utilizing peer- and self-editing checklists, rubrics, and language resources.**

1. Students should continue to work on the target areas of language usage as noted on their Language Usage Checklist (p. 129).

3. The short-answer practice provides a model for the short-answer items on the GED test, therefore, it is important that students do as much as they can from memory, however, referring to a grammar resource from time to time during practice should be fine.

4. After the writing is complete and students have evaluated the overall quality of their response with the checklist, they can edit it using the Editing Rubric (p. 131).

➢ Assessment & Next Steps

Students should complete the suggested practice activities and the activities included in each lesson. Evaluate which learning goals were not met and remediate by using other resources, such as those identified in the Bridging Knowledge section. Upon successful completion, continue to the next lesson.

DRAWING AND SUPPORTING CONCLUSIONS

Skills-Based Questions

1. What conclusions can you draw from the evidence presented in the text?

2. How can you share your conclusions in a well-supported response?

	Learning Goals:	GED
Knowledge Goals:	1. Describe the three steps used to present conclusions drawn from a text.	R.2.8
	2. Identify the evidence used to draw conclusions.	
Reading Goals:	1. Draw conclusions or make generalizations based on main ideas in text.	R.2.8
	2. Make logical inferences supported by evidence.	R.2.3
Vocabulary Goals:	1. Define key subject and academic vocabulary.	R.4.1
	2. Determine the meaning of unknown vocabulary using context clues, word forms, and parts of speech.	
	3. Produce writing and speech using new vocabulary.	
Written Response Goals:	1. Determine what is stated in the text and make logical inferences or conclusions supported by text evidence.	W.1
		W.2
	2. Respond to text by summarizing events clearly, organizing information logically, supporting conclusions with examples, and focusing on the writing task.	W.3
	3. Use standard English language conventions. *(See Language Usage Goals)*	
Language Usage Goals:	1. Use standard English grammar, punctuation, and mechanics.	W.3

Sample Instructional Support Strategies

➢ **Bridging Knowledge**

> **Strategy 1:** *Develop prior knowledge and skills to connect to new knowledge.*
>
> **Strategy 2:** *Use guiding questions to make connections beyond the lesson to broader life themes and topics.*
>
> **Strategy 3:** *Use reading strategies to develop, monitor, and synthesize new knowledge.* (See Bridging Reading)
>
> **Strategy 4:** *Demonstrate (and further develop) synthesis of new knowledge through written student response tasks.* (See Bridging Written Response)

1. Evaluate students' knowledge of the following language arts concepts and skills. Utilize the chart below to develop student background knowledge and skills as necessary.

Drawing and Supporting Conclusions	Reading Conclusions	Writing Conclusions	Language Usage
Writing for the GED Test Book 1: Grammar, Usage, and Mechanics			*Corresponding materials will vary based on the language usage area students choose to focus on.*
Core Skills in Reading & Writing	Unit 3, Lesson 4: Drawing Conclusions (p. 65)		
Scoreboost: Writing Across the Tests Sentence Structure, Usage, and Mechanics (SS); Responding to Text (RT)		RT: Communicate a Hypothesis or Conclusion (p. 35); Derive Evidence to Support a Conclusion (p. 37)	
Scoreboost: Thinking Skills Critical Thinking	Make Inferences (p. 8); Draw Conclusions (p. 20)		
Pre-HSE Workbook Reading (R); Writing 1 (W1); Writing 2 (W2)	R: Inferences and Conclusions (p. 14)		

2. Contextualize the Guided Practice portion of the lesson (p. 57) within a broader theme or topic by beginning the lesson with Guiding Questions. Guiding questions that are authentic and relevant to students draw them deeper into the lesson and allow them to build deeper knowledge beyond the content of the lesson.

> **Guiding Questions:**
>
> 1. What conclusions can you draw from the passage *The Geology of the Grand Canyon*?
>
> 2. What evidence can you use to support your conclusion?

➢ **Bridging Reading**

> **Strategy 1:** Determine the type of text, establish reading purpose, and make predictions using text features and signal words.
>
> **Strategy 2:** Develop text analysis using think-alouds, annotation, sentence frames, and graphic organizers.
>
> **Strategy 3:** Overcome text analysis barriers using prior knowledge, analyzing language usage, and using resources.
>
> **Strategy 4:** Synthesize text analysis using paraphrasing, text frames, graphic organizers, and peer discussions.

1. Students need to "unpack" the test item prompt to determine the purpose of the reading task. They can then scan the text for text features and signal words to determine the type of text and its purpose.

Guided Practice:	*The Geology of the Grand Canyon*
Test Prompt:	The Colorado River flows through the Grand Canyon. Based on the information in the passage, what can you <u>conclude</u> about the <u>current volume of water</u> that flows through the Grand Canyon? <u>Include</u> multiple pieces of <u>evidence</u> from the passage to support your answer.
Reading Purpose:	Draw conclusions from the passage about the current volume of water in the Grand Canyon and support it with evidence.
Text Purpose:	Informational

2. The lesson Drawing and Supporting Conclusions provides a three-step process for students to support conclusions they draw from science passages on the GED test. Step 1 in this process is Read and Analyze the Passage. As part of this step, the lesson suggests that students skim the passage for the overall main idea and key ideas that support possible conclusions. Students should outline the events that lead to the formation of the Grand Canyon and then determine what these events tell us about the current volume of water flowing through the Grand Canyon. Students should restate part of the writing prompt within their conclusion (see bolded text below).

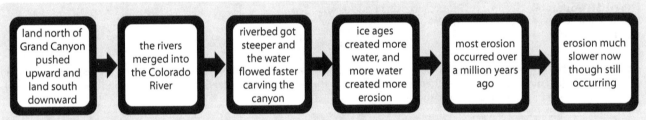

Conclusion: There is less erosion now so **the volume of water that flows through the Grand Canyon** must be less.

3. Continue to have students use the five-step process to figure out confusing words and areas of the text as in previous lessons.

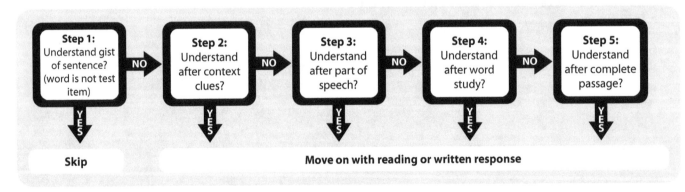

4. Students should outline the events in Strategy 2 using their own words. This sets them up for quicker paraphrasing for their response.

➤ Bridging Vocabulary

1. First, present the shortest form of the word (the base word, often the verb form), followed by other commonly used word forms (if available). Examine prefixes and suffixes and their impact on word meaning and usage.

2. Read the word as used in the context of the text and discuss possible meanings given context clues and word form.

3. Have students find (electronically or in print) the definition or translation of the base form and, if different, the form used in context and note these definitions for future reference and study.

4. Gradually build a deeper knowledge of the word by having students use the word in a sentence frame, guided discussion, and an original sentence (see Appendix D, p. 144).

➤ Bridging Written Response

Strategy 1: *Prepare for a response task by identifying its purpose, audience, signal words, structure, and style.*

Strategy 2: *Organize text analysis for written response using a graphic organizer and/or paragraph/essay frame.*

Strategy 3: *Overcome barriers to producing clear/coherent writing by using models, language analysis, and resources.*

Strategy 4: *Revise writing by utilizing peer- and self-editing checklists, rubrics, and writing resources.*

Strategy 5: *Extend text analysis to build upon initial information or claims by using evidence from additional sources.*

1. Students have already determined the purpose of the writing task in Bridging Reading Strategy 1. Now they should consider some signal words that match the purpose. Since the task is to draw conclusions, obviously signal words for conclusions will be helpful. Similarly, since the topic is science-related, cause and effect and sequencing signal words may be helpful.

Signal Words	Conclusion: *therefore, thus, in conclusion, as such, given, for this reason*
	Cause/effect: *due to, since, in order to, because of, therefore, consequently, as a result*
	Process/sequence: *First, second, next, then, after, since, prior to, during, finally*

2. Step 2 in the three-step process for drawing a conclusion is Plan and Write. Students need to organize their ideas in a way that fits the conventions of the writing purpose. For this writing task, a supported conclusion is required. Students should start with their conclusion, summarize the events that led them to that conclusion and how those events support their conclusion. Finally, they should end with a restatement of the conclusion. After students organize their ideas, they should successfully be able to write a short answer drawing a conclusion about the water volume in the Grand Canyon.

Conclusion:
Event 1:
Event 2:
Event 3:
Event 4:
Event 5:
Event 6:
Restate Conclusion:

3. Continue to stress that students will need to use their knowledge of vocabulary and language usage to construct their written responses on the GED test. If they can think back to a grammar or vocabulary activity or visualize one of their vocabulary or grammar resources, it may help them retrieve information from their memory and enable them to apply it to the task at hand.

4. Have students use a simple checklist to complete Step 3: Check and Revise.

   - Did I correctly identify my conclusion?

   - Did I give at least three details that support my conclusion?

   - Did I use my own words?

   - Does my writing sound fluent?

   - Is my writing clear?

➢ Bridging Language Usage

Strategy 1: Determine and target areas of language usage that require further development.

Strategy 2: Analyze specific areas of language usage as modeled in authentic and relevant communication tasks.

Strategy 3: Develop specific areas of language usage through participation in authentic communication tasks.

Strategy 4: Revise language usage by utilizing peer- and self-editing checklists, rubrics, and language resources.

1. Students should continue to work on the target areas of language usage as noted on their Language Usage Checklist (p. 129).

3. The short-answer practice provides a model for the short-answer items on the GED test, therefore, it is important that students do as much as they can from memory, however, referring to a grammar resource from time to time during practice should be fine.

4. After the writing is complete and students have evaluated the overall quality of their response with the checklist, they can edit it using the Editing Rubric (p. 131).

➢ Assessment & Next Steps

Students should complete the suggested practice activities and the activities included in each lesson. Evaluate which learning goals were not met and remediate by using other resources, such as those identified in the Bridging Knowledge section. Upon successful completion, continue to the next lesson.

CREATING AN EXPERIMENTAL DESIGN

Skills-Based Questions

1. What are the most common steps in the experimental design process (scientific method)?

2. How do you design an experiment to test a hypothesis?

	Learning Goals:	**GED**
Knowledge Goals:	1. Describe the steps in the experimental design process.	SP.2.d
	2. Identify steps to follow when testing a hypothesis.	
Reading Goals:	1. Identify hypotheses for scientific investigations.	SP.2.b
	2. Identify independent and dependent variables in scientific investigations.	SP.2.e
Vocabulary Goals:	1. Define key subject and academic vocabulary.	R.4.1
	2. Determine the meaning of unknown vocabulary using context clues, word forms, and parts of speech.	
	3. Produce writing and speech using new vocabulary.	
Written Response Goals:	1. Design a scientific investigation.	SP.2.d
	2. Describe the independent and dependent variables in scientific investigations.	SP.2.e
	3. Use standard English language conventions in writing. *(See Language Usage Goals)*	W.3
Language Usage Goals:	1. Use standard English grammar, punctuation, and mechanics.	W.3

Sample Instructional Support Strategies

> ## Bridging Knowledge

Strategy 1: *Develop prior knowledge and skills to connect to new knowledge.*

Strategy 2: *Use guiding questions to make connections beyond the lesson to broader life themes and topics.*

Strategy 3: *Use reading strategies to develop, monitor, and synthesize new knowledge.* (See Bridging Reading)

Strategy 4: *Demonstrate (and further develop) synthesis of new knowledge through written student response tasks.*
(See Bridging Written Response)

1. Evaluate students' knowledge of the following language arts concepts and skills. Utilize the chart below to develop student background knowledge and skills as necessary.

Creating an Experimental Design	Reading Experimental Design	Writing Experimental Design	Language Usage Choose focus area
Writing for the GED Test Book 1: Grammar, Usage, and Mechanics			Corresponding materials will vary based on the language usage area students choose to focus on.
Core Skills in Science	Unit 1, Lesson 1: Investigation Design (p. 13)		
Scoreboost: Writing Across the Tests Sentence Structure, Usage, and Mechanics (SS); Responding to Text (RT)		RT: Communicate a Hypothesis or Conclusion (p. 35); Derive Evidence to Support a Conclusion (p. 37)	
Pre-HSE Workbook: Science		Hypotheses (p. 20); Experimental Design (p. 26)	

> ## Bridging Reading

Strategy 1: *Determine the type of text, establish reading purpose, and make predictions using text features and signal words.*

Strategy 2: *Develop text analysis using think-alouds, annotation, sentence frames, and graphic organizers.*

Strategy 3: *Overcome text analysis barriers using prior knowledge, analyzing language usage, and using resources.*

Strategy 4: *Synthesize text analysis using paraphrasing, text frames, graphic organizers, and peer discussions.*

1. First, students should skim the test prompt in the lesson (p. 59) to determine their reading purpose. Then they will need to "unpack" the directions portion to determine the purpose of their writing task. Students will analyze the descriptive part of the prompt in Strategy 2.

Test Prompt:		
Directions: *Design a controlled experiment that the math specialist can use to test her hypothesis. Be sure to include how data will be collected and how the results will be analyzed.*		
Action	**What?**	**How or Why?**
Design	controlled experiment	to test her hypothesis
Include	how data will be collected and how results will be analyzed	

2. Students will now "unpack" the description of the writing prompt to identify the hypothesis and the two sides of its "if-(then)" relationship.

> **Test Prompt:**
>
> **Description:** A math specialist has designed a software tutorial program that she believes will help struggling students score better on a standardized state math test. She hypothesizes that if struggling students use her program three hours a week for six months, they will see their test scores increase by an average of 10 percentage points.

➤ Bridging Vocabulary

> ***Strategy 1: Identify the component parts and usage of new words to interpret their meanings.***
>
> ***Strategy 2: Use context clues to interpret new words, including figurative and connotative language.***
>
> ***Strategy 3: Utilize vocabulary-building resources.***
>
> ***Strategy 4: Build a deeper knowledge of words through writing and speaking tasks.***

1. First, present the shortest form of the word (the base word, often the verb form), followed by other commonly used word forms (if available). Examine prefixes and suffixes and their impact on word meaning and usage.

2. Read the word as used in the context of the text and discuss possible meanings given context clues and word form.

3. Have students find (electronically or in print) the definition or translation of the base form and, if different, the form used in context and note these definitions for future reference and study.

4. Gradually build a deeper knowledge of the word by having students use the word in a sentence frame, guided discussion, and an original sentence (see Appendix D, p. 144).

➤ Bridging Written Response

> ***Strategy 1: Prepare for a response task by identifying its purpose, audience, signal words, structure, and style.***
>
> ***Strategy 2: Organize text analysis for written response using a graphic organizer and/or paragraph/essay frame.***
>
> ***Strategy 3: Overcome barriers to producing clear/coherent writing by using models, language analysis, and resources.***
>
> ***Strategy 4: Revise writing by utilizing peer- and self-editing checklists, rubrics, and writing resources.***
>
> ***Strategy 5: Extend text analysis to build upon initial information or claims by using evidence from additional sources.***

1. Students have already determined the purpose of the writing task in Bridging Reading Strategy 1. Now they should consider the structure of a scientific experiment. The experiment should have the following components:

   1. a statement of the hypothesis,

   2. a description of the experiment,

   3. a description of data collection, and

   4. a description of data analysis.

   The experiment description should identify both an experimental group and a control group as well as the the independent, dependent, and control variables.

   In addition, students should prepare a list of signal words.

Signal Words	Process/sequence: *first, second, next, then, after, since, prior to, during, finally*
	Cause/effect: *due to, since, in order to, because of, therefore, consequently, as a result*
	Compare/contrast: *likewise, similarly, similar to, equally, unlike, differ, in contrast, however, on the other hand*

2. Next students can plan their response by organizing the components of an experiment using a graphic organizer similar to this one.

Hypothesis: struggling students who use the math tutorial program for 3 hours a week for 6 months will increase their test scores by 10% on average.		
Experiment Description		
Experimental Group: *Students using the math tutorial program*		**Control Group:** *Students not using the math tutorial program*
Dependent Variable *Math test scores*	**Independent Variable** *Math tutorial program*	**Control Variable** *Level of students: struggling in math Length of instruction (3 hours a week for 6 months)*
Data Collection: pre-test before instruction; post-test after instruction		
Data Analysis: determine the percentage increase between pre- and post-test scores for each group; compare average increase in scores between the two groups.		

3. From here, students can construct the written response, using complete sentences to describe each part of the experimental design as presented in the graphic organizer. Continue to stress that students will need to use their knowledge of vocabulary and language conventions to construct their written responses on the GED test. If they can think back to a grammar or vocabulary activity or visualize one of their vocabulary or grammar resources, it may help them retrieve information from their memory and enable them to apply it to the task at hand.

4. Have students use a simple checklist to Check and Revise their written response.

   • Did I correctly identify the hypothesis?

   • Did I identify the experimental and control groups correctly?

   • Did I identify the dependent, independent, and control variables correctly?

   • Did I include data collection and data analysis information?

   • Does my writing sound fluent and clear?

   Note: Have students repeat the Bridging Reading and Bridging Written Response strategies with the Guided Practice writing prompt on page 61 of *Writing* book 3.

➢ Bridging Language Usage

Strategy 1: **Determine and target areas of language usage that require further development.**

Strategy 2: *Analyze specific areas of language usage as modeled in authentic and relevant communication tasks.*

Strategy 3: **Develop specific areas of language usage through participation in authentic communication tasks.**

Strategy 4: **Revise language usage by utilizing peer and self editing checklists and rubrics and language resources.**

1. Students should continue to work on the target areas of language usage as noted on their Language Usage Checklist (p. 129).

3. The short-answer practice provides a model for the short-answer items on the GED test, therefore, it is important that students do as much as they can from memory, however, referring to a grammar resource from time to time during practice should be fine.

4. After the writing is complete and students have evaluated the overall quality of their response with the checklist, they can edit it by using the Editing Rubric (p. 131).

➢ Assessment & Next Steps

Students should complete the suggested practice activities and the activities included in each lesson. Evaluate which learning goals were not met and remediate by using other resources, such as those identified in the Bridging Knowledge section.

Language Usage Resources

LANGUAGE USAGE CHECKLIST

Goal Set (Date)	Language Area	Required Skills (Can use simple annotation)		Skill Mastered (Date)
Sentence Structure				
	1. Simple sentences	a.	Identify main subjects and verbs.	
		b.	Include correct capitalization and ending punctuation.	
	2. Compound sentences	a.	Identify subjects and verbs.	
		b.	Include coordinating conjunction with comma.	
		c.	Include correct capitalization and ending punctuation.	
	3. Complex sentences	a.	Identify subjects and verbs.	
		b.	Include subordinating conjunction (with comma if at beginning of sentence).	
		c.	Include correct capitalization and ending punctuation.	
	4. Sentence Fragments	a.	Identify subjects and verbs.	
		d.	Identify subordinating conjunctions.	
		b.	Include correct capitalization and ending punctuation.	
	5. Run-ons and comma splices	a.	Identify subjects and verbs.	
		b.	Include coordinating conjunction with comma.	
		c.	Include semicolon without coordinating conjunction.	
		d.	Include correct capitalization and ending punctuation.	
	6. Parallelism and coordination	a.	Include correct coordinating conjunctions.	
		b.	Use same form for words and phrases on each side of coordinating conjunction.	
		c.	Use same form for a list of words or phrases.	
	7. Misplaced and dangling modifiers	a.	Identify prepositional phrases and adjective/adverb clauses.	
		b.	Identify what the phrase/clause describes.	
		c.	Put phrases and clauses next to what they modify.	
		d.	Include what is being modified in the sentence.	

Goal Set (Date)	Language Area	Required Skills (Can use simple annotation)	Skill Mastered (Date)
Grammar and Usage			
	1. Nouns and pronouns	a. Identify nouns in subject and object positions.	
		b. Include correct pronouns in subject and object positions.	
		c. Make pronouns agree with nouns in number.	
	2. Possessives and relative pronouns	a. Use possessive pronouns correctly with/without nouns.	
		b. Include apostrophes with possessive nouns.	
		c. Identify relative clauses and use restrictive ones with a comma and nonrestrictive ones without.	
	3. Verb tenses and forms	a. Use simple verb tenses in past, present, and future.	
		b. Use continuous verb tenses in past, present, and future.	
		c. Include correct verb form for person and number.	
		d. Form irregular verbs correctly in the simple past tense.	
	4. Perfect tenses	a. Use perfect verb tenses in past, present, and future.	
		b. Form irregular verbs correctly in perfect verb tenses.	
	5. Subject-verb agreement	a. Identify subjects and verbs.	
		b. Switch order of subject and verbs in questions.	
		c. Make verbs agree with subjects in person and number.	
		d. Make verbs agree with indefinite pronouns in number.	
	6. Pronouns and antecedents	a. Identify pronouns and antecedents.	
		b. Make pronouns and antecedents agree in number.	
		c. Include a clear antecedent.	
	7. Informal and nonstandard usage	a. Identify informal and nonstandard English.	
		b. Change informal and nonstandard English to formal, standard English.	
	8. Wordy and awkward writing	a. Revise wordy writing (Is this necessary for my point?)	
		b. Revise awkward writing. (Does this sound good aloud?)	
Mechanics			
	1. Capitalization	Include correct capitalization: First letter of a sentence and a proper noun.	
	2. Commas	Include commas after: coordinating conjunctions, a clause at the beginning of a sentence, and items in a list.	
	3. Semicolons	Include semicolon for a compound sentence without a coordinating conjunction or with a conjunctive adverb.	
	4. Plurals and possessives	Include the correct plural form (spelling) of nouns and possessive nouns (apostrophe placement).	
	5. Words that sound alike	Use words that sound alike correctly in meaning and spelling.	

EDITING RUBRIC

Author: _____   Editor: _____   Date: _____

1. Read the text.
2. Read the questions below and follow the corresponding action.
3. Check the level of performance for each item using the boxes on the right.

Questions Did the author:	Editor Action You need to:	Level of Performance		
		Rarely 0–49%	Often 50–79%	Usually 80–100%
1. Write complete sentences?	a. Identify subjects and verbs b. Check capitalization and ending punctuation c. Mark errors			
2. Include correctly formed compound and complex sentences?	a. Identify subjects, verbs and coordinating and subordinating conjunctions b. Check comma and semicolon placement c. Check capitalization and ending punctuation d. Mark errors			
3. Use correct verb tense with correctly formed verbs?	a. Identify verbs and appropriate tense b. Check verbs for correct form and spelling			
4. Make all verbs and subjects agree?	a. Identify subjects and verbs b. Check agreement of each c. Check agreement with indefinite pronouns d. Mark errors			
5. Use the right form of all pronouns?	a. Identify pronouns in the subject and object position and check the form of each b. Identify the noun each pronoun replaces and check agreement of each c. Mark errors			
6. Use possessives correctly?	a. Identify possessive pronouns and nouns b. Check form of possessive pronouns c. Check apostrophe placement of possessive nouns			
7. Include pronouns and antecedents that agree?	a. Identify pronouns and their antecedents b. Check that they are clear and agree			
8. Use modifiers correctly?	a. Identify phrases and clauses and what they describe (modify) b. Mark unclear modifiers (phrases/clauses)			
9. Avoid wordy and awkward writing?	a. Identify areas that are too wordy or confusing b. Mark these areas			
10. Avoid informal and nonstandard English?	a. Identify informal and nonstandard uses of English b. Mark these areas			

EXTENDED-RESPONSE EVALUATION RUBRIC

Author: _____   Editor: _____   Date: _____

1. Read the text.
2. Read the questions below and follow the action to the right.
3. Check the level of performance for each item using the boxes on the right.

Question Did the author:	Editor Action You need to:	Level of Performance		
		No 0	Somewhat 1	Yes 2
1. State a clear central claim?	a. Underline the claim b. Note problems or suggestions			
2. Provide relevant and specific reasons?	a. Underline each sentence that introduces a new reason b. Note if it is relevant and specific (+) or not (-)			
3. Provide sufficient reasons? (2+ reasons for each argument)	a. Underline each sentence that introduces a new reason b. Count reasons and note if not sufficient			
4. Present sound reasons (no fallacies)?	a. Mark each reason as sound (+) or unsound (-) b. Note any fallacies* (see list below)			
5. Support reasons with reliable evidence?	a. Circle examples of evidence b. Mark as reliable (+) or unreliable (-) c. If unreliable**, note why (see list below)			
6. Include an introduction, body, and conclusion?	a. Place brackets around the introduction, body, and conclusion b. Note if any are missing			
7. Present ideas that are fully developed and supported with evidence from the text?	a. Review the underlined reasons and the circled evidence; each reason needs evidence to support it b. Note gaps in evidence			
8. Include only paragraphs that are related to the claim and are presented in logical order?	a. Note if any sentences or paragraphs do not relate to the claim			
9. Choose words that express ideas clearly, including signal words?	a. Identify areas that are too wordy or confusing b. Mark these areas with (?)			
10. Match his/her writing to the audience and purpose of the task?	a. Identify informal and nonstandard uses of English b. Mark these areas and make suggestions			

* Fallacies of Logic: 1) Jump on the Bandwagon 2) Personal Attack 3) Either/Or Thinking 4) Slippery Slope

** Unreliable Evidence: 1) Not knowledgeable source 2) Biased source 3) Outdated information

LANGUAGE USAGE CROSS-REFERENCE GUIDE

LANGUAGE USAGE AREA	Writing for the GED Test Book 1: Grammar, Usage and Mechanics	Writing for the GED Test Book 2: Reading Comprehension	Writing for the GED Test Book 3: Extended Response and Short Answers	Scoreboost: Writing Across the Tests: Sentence Structure, Usage, and Mechanics	Pre-HSE Workbook: Writing 1	Core Skills in Reading & Writing: Unit 4, Grammar and Usage
Sentence Structure						
1. Simple sentences	Basic Sentence Parts, p. 20; Simple and Compound Sentences, p. 22	Main Ideas and Supporting Details, p. 12 (*Bridging*, p. 22)	Analyzing Arguments, p. 12 (*Bridging*, p. 75); Summarizing a Science Passage, p. 52 (*Bridging*, p. 115); Sentence Structure, p. 36		Parts of a Sentence, p. 12; Complete Sentences, p. 34	Parts of Speech, p. 80; Sentence Structure, p. 84
2. Compound sentences	Simple and Compound Sentences, p. 22	Main Ideas and Supporting Details, p. 12 (*Bridging*, p. 22)	Evaluating Reasoning, p. 16 (*Bridging*, p. 79); Drawing and Supporting Conclusions, p. 54 (*Bridging*, p. 120); Sentence Variety, p. 37	Coordinate Ideas in Sentences, p. 6	Compound Sentences, p. 36; Sentence Variety, p. 46	Types of Sentences, p. 88
3. Complex sentences	Complex Sentences, p. 24	Sequence of Events, p. 18 (*Bridging*, p. 28)	Evaluating Reasoning, p. 16 (*Bridging*, p. 79); Drawing and Supporting Conclusions, p. 54 (*Bridging*, p. 120); Sentence Variety, p. 37	Subordinate Ideas in Sentences, p. 8	Complex Sentences, p. 38; Sentence Variety, p. 46	Types of Sentences, p. 88
4. Sentence Fragments	Sentence Fragments, p. 26	Cause-and-Effect Relationships, p. 30 (*Bridging*, p. 39); Plot, p. 46 (*Bridging*, p. 51)	Analyzing Arguments, p. 12 (*Bridging*, p. 75); Summarizing a Science Passage, p. 52 (*Bridging*, p. 115); Sentence Structure, p. 36	Correct Sentence Fragments, p. 10	Sentence Fragments, p. 42	Types of Sentences, p. 88
5. Run-ons and comma splices	Run-ons and Comma Splices, p. 28	Language: Meaning and Tone, p. 36 (*Bridging*, p. 45); Plot, p. 46 (*Bridging*, p. 51)	Analyzing Arguments, p. 12 (*Bridging*, p. 75); Summarizing a Science Passage, p. 52 (*Bridging*, p. 115); Sentence Structure, p. 36	Correct Run-Ons and Fused Sentences, p. 4	Run-Ons and Comma Splices, p. 40	Types of Sentences, p. 88
6. Parallelism and coordination	Parallelism and Coordination, p. 30	Character, p. 52 (*Bridging*, p. 56)		Coordinate Ideas in Sentences, p. 6; Make Ideas Parallel, p. 14	Parallel Form, p. 44	
7. Misplaced and dangling modifiers	Misplaced Modifiers, p. 32; Dangling Modifiers, p. 34	Theme, p. 58 (*Bridging*, p. 61)		Use Modifiers Correctly, p. 12		

Grammar and Usage

LANGUAGE USAGE AREA	Writing for the GED Test Book 1: Grammar, Usage and Mechanics	Writing for the GED Test Book 2: Reading Comprehension	Writing for the GED Test Book 3: Extended Response and Short Answers	Scoreboost: Writing Across the Tests: Sentence Structure, Usage, and Mechanics	Pre-HSE Workbook: Writing 1	Core Skills in Reading & Writing: Unit 4, Grammar and Usage
1. Nouns and pronouns	Basic Sentence Parts, p. 20 — Nouns and Personal Pronouns, p. 38	Inferences and Conclusions, p. 6 (*Bridging*, p. 16)	Practice the RLA Extended Response, p. 46 (*Bridging*, p. 110) — Pronoun Form and Agreement, p. 39	Correct Errors in Pronoun Usage, p. 24	Nouns and Plurals, p. 14 — Pronouns, p. 18	Parts of Speech, p. 80
2. Possessives and relative pronouns	Other Kinds of Pronouns, p. 40	Comparisons and Contrasts, p. 24 (*Bridging*, p. 33)	Practice the RLA Extended Response, p. 46 (*Bridging*, p. 110) — Pronoun Form and Agreement, p. 39	Correct Errors in Pronoun Usage, p. 24	Pronoun Agreement, p. 22	Agreement, p. 99
3. Verb tenses and forms	Verb Tenses and Forms, p. 42 — Irregular Verbs, p. 44	Inferences and Conclusions, p. 6 (*Bridging*, p. 16)			Basic Verb Tenses and Forms, p. 24 — Irregular Verbs, p. 26 — Progressive Tenses, p. 28	Verbs, p. 104
4. Perfect tenses	The Perfect Tenses, p. 46	Sequence of Events, p. 18 (*Bridging*, p. 28)				
5. Subject-verb agreement	Subject-Verb Agreement I, p. 48 — Subject-Verb Agreement II, p. 50 — Subject-Verb Agreement III, p. 52	Main Ideas and Supporting Details, p. 12 (*Bridging*, p. 22) — Sequence of Events, p. 18 (*Bridging*, p. 28) — Cause-and-Effect Relationships, p. 30 (*Bridging*, p. 39)	Creating an Experimental Design, p. 57 (*Bridging*, p. 125) — Subject-Verb Agreement, p. 38	Make Subjects and Verbs Agree, p. 20 — Make Subjects and Verbs Agree in Complicated Sentence Structures, p. 22	Subject-Verb Agreement, p. 30	Agreement, p. 99
6. Pronouns and antecedents	Pronoun-Antecedent Agreement, p. 54 — Clear Antecedents, p. 56	Character, p. 52 (*Bridging*, p. 56)		Fix Pronoun Agreement Problems, p. 26		Agreement, p. 99
7. Informal and nonstandard usage	Informal and Nonstandard Usage, p. 58	Figurative Language, p. 64 (*Bridging*, p. 67)				
8. Wordy and awkward writing	Wordy and Awkward Writing, p. 60	Figurative Language, p. 64 (*Bridging*, p. 67)		Edit or Eliminate Wordy or Awkward Sentences (p. 16)		

LANGUAGE USAGE AREA	Writing for the GED Test 1: Grammar, Usage and Mechanics	Writing for the GED Test Book 2: Reading Comprehension	Writing for the GED Test Book 3: Extended Response and Short Answers	Scoreboost: Writing Across the Tests: Sentence Structure, Usage, and Mechanics	Pre-HSE Workbook: Writing 1	Core Skills in Reading & Writing: Unit 4, Grammar and Usage
Mechanics						
1. Capitalization	Capitalization, p. 64	Figurative Language, p. 64 (*Bridging*, p. 67)	Analyzing Arguments, p. 12 (*Bridging*, p. 75) Summarizing a Science Passage, p. 52 (*Bridging*, p. 115) Capitalization, p. 42	Capitalize Correctly, p. 30	Capital Letters, p. 16	Capitalization, p. 104
2. Commas	Commas, p. 66	Sequence of Events, p. 18 (*Bridging*, p. 28) Cause-and-Effect Relationships, p. 30 (*Bridging*, p. 39) Language: Meaning and Tone, p. 36 (*Bridging*, p. 45)	Evaluating Reasoning, p. 16 (*Bridging*, p. 79) Drawing and Supporting Conclusions, p. 54 (*Bridging*, p. 120) Commas, p. 40	Use Commas Correctly, p. 32		Commas, p. 92
3. Semicolons	Semicolons, p. 68	Cause-and-Effect Relationships, p. 30 (*Bridging*, p. 39) Language: Meaning and Tone, p. 36 (*Bridging*, p. 45)		Capitalization, Punctuation, and Spelling, p. 36		Punctuation, p. 95
4. Plurals and possessives	Plurals and Possessives, p. 70	Theme, p. 58 (*Bridging*, p. 61)	Practice the RLA Extended Response, p. 46 (*Bridging*, p. 110) Apostrophes, p. 41	Capitalization, Punctuation, and Spelling, p. 36	Nouns and Plurals, p. 14 Possessives, p. 20	Punctuation, p. 95
5. Words that sound alike	Words That Sound Alike, p. 72	Figurative Language, p. 64 (*Bridging*, p. 67)	Creating an Experimental Design, p. 57 (*Bridging*, p. 125) Words That Sound Alike, p. 43	Spell Well, p. 34	Spelling, p. 32	Spelling, p. 108

Language for Specific Purposes

SIGNAL WORDS

Purpose	Language
Cause	due to, since, in order to, because of, as, so as to, so that, given that
Effect	therefore, consequently, as a result, then, for this reason, thus
Conclusion	therefore, thus, in conclusion, as such, given, for this reason
Demonstrate	this, that, here, there, above, below The diagram … shows, illustrates, represents, charts
Examples	for example, such as, including, like, one example is, for instance, in other words, to illustrate
Summary	in summary, to summarize, overall, to sum up, on the whole, in general
Compare	likewise, similarly, same as, like, similar to, equally
Contrast	unlike, differ, different from, in contrast, however, on the other hand
Definitions	is defined as, means, is called, referred to as
Emphasize	main, key, critical, important, integral, especially, truly, namely
Process/Sequence	first, second, next, then, after, since, prior to, during, finally
Support	important to note, another important point, in fact, not only … but also, as a matter of fact, furthermore, additionally, also

DISCOURSE PROMPTS

Purpose	Language
Contribute to the Group	I think ____ because ____. I believe we should ____ because ____. My idea is that ____. Let's ____ so that ____.
Encourage Participation	What do you think? I'd like to hear what you have to say about ____. Do you have anything to add? We haven't heard from ____.
Present Evidence	An example of this is ____. ____ is an example of ____. According to the text/author ____. The text/author says here ____. The graph shows ___.
Disagree Politely	I see what you're saying, but ____. Another way to think about this is ____. Have you thought about ____? I think there's another way to look at that.
Paraphrase Contributions	So, do we agree that ____? I think you're saying ____. It sounds like we agree that ____. If I understand correctly, ____.
Probe Others' Contributions	Could you explain that further? What did you mean by ____? Can you give me an example of what you mean? Can you support what you're saying with evidence?

LANGUAGE FOR TEST-TAKING

Verbs		Nouns	
analyze	interact	analysis	idea (central/main)
calculate	interpret	bias	inferences (logical)
cause	label	cause	information (numerical/technical)
compare	make	cause-and-effect	judgment
correlate	predict	circumstances	label
describe	recognize	claim	meaning
determine	show	claims (valid)	opinion
develop	support	connection	order (chronological)
identify		context	point of view
		correlation	propaganda
		data	purpose
		details	result
		effect	sources (primary/secondary)
		evidence	trend
		fact	variable (independent/dependent)
		hypothesis (hypotheses)	

Vocabulary Development Lists

Academic words are broken down by syllables. Alternate uses of the academic words show the prefix or suffix in italics.

Writing for the GED Test 2: Reading Comprehension

Reading Informational Texts

Inferences and Conclusions
Content Words
author
biography
clue
conclusion
   [conclude]
detail
draw (conclusions)
imply
inference
   [infer]
informational
   [inform]
memoir
nonfiction
purpose (author's purpose)
text

Academic Words
1. confine (verb)   [con • fine]
   confine*ment* (noun)
2. content (verb/noun)   [con • tént/cón • tent]
   content*ment* (noun)
3. feeble (adjective)   [fee • ble]
4. genius (noun/adjective)   [gen • ius]
5. prostrate (verb/adjective)   [pros • trate]
6. scatter (verb)   [scat • ter]
7. suffer (verb)   [suf • fer]
8. venture (verb/noun)   [ven • ture]

Main Ideas and Supporting Details
Content Words
description
   [describe]
heading
main (idea)
paragraph
quotation
   [quote]
section
statistic
supporting (details)
   [support]
topic (sentence)
transition

Academic Words
1. benefit (noun/verb)   [ben • e • fit]
   beneficial (adjective)
2. devastate (verb)   [dev • as • tate]
   devasta*tion* (noun)
   devastat*ing* (adjective)
3. drought (noun)   [drought]
4. interact (verb)   [in • ter • act]
   interac*tion* (noun)
   interac*tive* (adjective)
5. mutual (adjective)   [mu • tu • al]
   mutual*ism* (noun)
6. severe (adjective)   [se • vere]
   sever*ity* (noun)
7. symbiosis (noun)   [sym • bi • o • sis]
   symbio*tic* (adjective)
8. threat (noun)   [threat]
   threat*en* (verb)
   threaten*ing* (adjective)

Sequence of Events
Content Words
chronological
   [chronology]
organization
   [organize]
pattern
sequence (of events)
sequential (order)
signal (words)

Academic Words
1. active (verb)   [ac • tive]
   activ*ity* (noun)
2. during (preposition)   [dur • ing]
3. endure (verb)   [en • dure]
   endur*ance* (noun)
4. expedite (verb)   [ex • pe • dite]
   exped*ition* (noun)
5. final (noun/adjective)   [fi • nal]
   final*ly* (adjective)
6. meanwhile (adverb)   [mean • while]
7. stage (noun/verb)   [stage]
8. struggle (verb/noun)   [strug • gle]

Comparisons and Contrasts
Content Words
compare
   [comparison]
contrast
Venn diagram

similar
  [similarity]
block (style)
point-by-point (structure)

Academic Words

1. agree (verb)   [a • gree]
     agree*ment* (noun)
     agree*able* (adjective)
2. approach (verb/noun)   [ap • proach]
     approach*able* (adjective)
3. counsel (verb/noun)   [coun • sel]
4. oppose (verb)   [op • pose]
     oppos*ition* (noun)
     oppos*ite* (adjective/noun)
5. reform (verb/noun)   [re • form]
6. respond (verb)   [re • spond]
     respon*se* (noun)
7. restore (verb)   [re • store]
     restor*ation* (noun)
8. unlike (adverb/preposition)   [un • like]

Cause-and-Effect Relationships
Content Words

causal (chain)
cause
effect
multiple
relationship
  [relate]
result

Academic Words

1. affect (noun)   [af • fect]
2. condition (noun)   [con • di • tion]
     condition*al* (adjective)
3. depend (verb)   [de • pend]
     depend*ence* (noun)
     depend*able* (adjective)
     depend*ent* (adjective/noun)
4. impact (verb/noun)   [im • pact]
5. improve (verb)   [im • prove]
     improve*ment* (noun)
6. provide (verb)   [pro • vide]
7. trigger (verb/noun)   [trig • ger]
8. result (verb/noun)   [re • sult]

Language: Meaning and Tone
Content Words

associate
  [association]
attitude
connotation
  [connote]
context
  [contextual; contextualize]
denotation
  [denote]

literal
negative
neutral
positive
straightforward
tone

Academic Words

1. colossal (adjective)   [co • los • sal]
2. fringe (noun)   [fringe]
3. gallant (adjective)   [gal • lant]
     gallant*ry* (noun)
4. imperial (adjective)   [im • pe • ri • al]
5. impose (verb)   [im • pose]
     impos*ing* (adjective)
     impos*ition* (noun)
6. lurid (adjective)   [lu • rid]
7. slouch (verb)   [slouch]
8. tumble (verb)   [tum • ble]

Plot
Content Words

character
  [characterize; characterization]
climax
  [climactic]
conflict
excerpt
exposition
falling action
fiction
  [fictional]
plot
resolution
  [resolve]
rising action
setting

Academic Words

1. conflict (verb/noun)   [con • flíct/cón • flict]
2. despair (verb/noun)   [de • spair]
     desper*ate* (adjective)
     despera*tion* (noun)
3. discover (verb)   [dis • cov • er]
     discover*y* (noun)
4. disappear (verb)   [dis • ap • pear]
     disappear*ance* (noun)
5. fulfill (verb)   [ful • fill]
     fulfill*ment* (adjective)
6. happen (verb)   [hap • pen]
7. scold (verb)   [scold]
     scold*ing* (noun)
8. suspect (verb)   [sus • pect]
     susp*icion* (noun)
     suspic*ious* (adjective)

Character
Content Words

convey
impression
motivation
    [motivate]
narrator
    [narrate]
trait

Academic Words

1. agony (noun)   [ag • o • ny]
        ago*nize* (verb)
2. blush (verb)   [blush]
3. crimson (noun/adjective)   [crim • son]
4. deficit (noun)   [def • i • cit]
        defic*ient* (adjective)
5. express (verb)   [ex • press]
        express*ion* (noun)
        express*ive* (adjective)
6. haste (noun)   [haste]
        hast*en* (verb)
7. possess (verb)   [pos • sess]
        posses*sion* (noun)
        posses*sive* (adjective)
8. tremble (verb)   [trem • ble]

Theme
Content Words

experience
fable
insight
lesson
message
outcome
response
    [respond]
theme
    [thematic]
traditional

Academic Words

1. aghast (adjective)   [a • ghast]
2. agitate (verb)   [ag • i • tate]
        agita*tion* (noun)
3. brilliant (adjective)   [bril • liant]
        brilli*ance* (noun)
4. cower (verb)   [cow • er]
5. dare (verb)   [dare]
        dar*ing* (adjective/noun)
6. portray (verb)   [por • tray]
        portray*al* (noun)
7. radiate (verb)   [ra • di • ate]
        radi*ance* (noun)
        radi*ant* (adjective)
8. rare (adjective)   [rare]
        rar*ity* (noun)

Figurative Language
Content Words

exaggeration
    [exaggerate]
figurative (language)
human (qualities)
hyperbole
imaginative (comparison)
    [image; imagine; imagination]
metaphor
personification
simile
symbolism
    [symbol; symbolic]

Academic Words

1. chill (verb/noun)   [chill]
        chill*ed* (adjective)
2. curious (adjective)   [cu • ri • ous]
        curios*ity* (noun)
3. dread (verb/noun)   [dread]
        dread*ful* (adjective)
        dread*ed* (adjective)
4. engulf (verb)   [en • gulf]
        engulf*ed* (adjective)
5. jostle (verb)   [jos • tle]
6. moist (adjective)   [moist]
        moist*en* (verb)
        moist*ure* (noun)
7. tempest (noun)   [tem • pest]
        tempest*uous* (adjective)
8. torrent (noun)   [tor • rent]
        torrent*ial* (adjective)

Writing for the GED Test Book 3: Extended Response and Short Answers

Introduction to Extended Response
Content Words

prompt
rubric
passage
argument
persuade
    [persuasive; persuasion]
editorial
evidence
development
    [develop]
structure
clarity
    [clarify; clarification]
convention
command
analyze
    [analysis]
revise
    [revision]

Academic Words

Not applicable (no reading passage featured in this lesson)

Read and Analyze
Content Words

assertion
    [assert]
claim
counterargument
expert (opinion)
judgment
    [judge]
opinion
position
refute
specific
    [specify]
statistic
valid (claim; argument)

Academic Words

1. contribute (verb)   [con • trib • ute]
    contribu*tion* (noun)
2. convince (verb)   [con • vince]
3. current (adjective)   [cur • rent]
    current*ly* (adverb)
4. drawback (noun)   [draw • back]
5. however (adverb)   [how • ev • er]
6. opponent (noun)   [op • po • nent]
7. proponent (noun)   [pro • po • nent]
8. predict (verb)   [pre • dict]
    predict*ion* (noun)
9. promise (verb/noun)   [prom • ise]
    promis*ing* (adjective)

Evaluating Reasoning
Content Words

attack (personal…)
bandwagon (jump on the…)
bias
    [biased]
fallacies
    [fallacy]
knowledgeable
    [knowledge]
logical
    [logic]
relevant
reliable
    [rely]
slippery slope
sound
source
specific
    [specify]
unbiased
up to date

Academic Words

1. advocate (verb/noun-person) [ad • vo • cate]
    advocac*y* (noun)
2. argue (verb)   [ar • gue]
    argu*ment* (noun)
3. consume (verb)   [con • sume]
    consump*tion* (noun)
    consum*er* (noun-person)
4. illustrate (verb)   [il • lus • trate]
    illustra*tion* (noun)
5. lead to (verb)   [lead to]
6. serious (adjective)   [se • ri • ous]
7. solve (verb)   [solve]
    sol*ution* (noun)
8. temporary (adjective)   [tem • po • ra • ry]

Characteristics of Good Responses
Content Words

argument
awareness
    [aware]
blog post
characteristic
claim
development
    [develop]
editorial
evidence
extended (response)
    [extend]
introduction
    [introduce]
progression (logical…)
    [progress]
response
    [respond]
signal words
support
    [supporting]
transition

Academic Words

1. admit (verb)   [ad • mit]
    admis*sion* (noun)
2. assume (verb)   [as • sume]
    assump*tion* (noun)
3. convince (verb)   [con • vince]
    convinc*ing* (verb)
4. in contrast (preposition-noun) [in con • trast]
5. in favor (preposition-noun) [in fa • vor]
6. quality (noun)   [qual • i • ty]
7. support (verb/noun)   [sup • port]
    support*ing* (adjective)
    support*ive* (adjective)
8. suit (verb)   [suit]
    suit*able* (adjective)
    *un*suit*able* (adjective)

Plan: Determine Your Claim and Evidence
Content Words

claim
counterargument
determine
evidence
gather
reasons
refute
relevant
reliable
sound
specific
sufficient

Academic Words

Not applicable (no reading passage featured in this lesson)

Plan: Organize Your Response
Content Words

audience
background
body
conclusion
introduction
    [introduce]
paragraph
provide
state
    [restate]
summary
topic

Academic Words

Not applicable (no reading passage featured in this lesson)

Plan: Create a Progression of Ideas
Content Words

ascending (order)
    [ascend]
block (style)
descending (order)
    [descend]
elaborate
main point
paragraph (development)
progression (of ideas)
    [progress]
sequence
    [sequential]
support
topic sentence
transition (words)

Academic Words

Not applicable (no reading passage featured in this lesson)

Write a Response
Content Words

See content words from previous lessons.

Academic Words

Not applicable (no reading passage featured in this lesson)

Check and Revise
Content Words

See Language Usage Checklist (p. 129) for a complete list of sentence structure, grammar, and mechanics terms.

Academic Words

Not applicable (no reading passage featured in this lesson)

Timed Extended-Response Practice
Content Words

See content words from previous lessons.

Academic Words

Note: If you plan to utilize this lesson as an authentic practice for the GED extended response then you will not want to pre-teach this list of vocabulary to your students. Instead, they will need to use their vocabulary strategies to interpret unknown words and phrases in the text.

1. alternate (verb/noun)   [al • ter • nate]
    alterna*tive* (adjective)
2. avoid (verb)   [a • void]
    avoid*ance* (noun)
    avoid*able* (adjective)
3. damage (noun)   [dam • age]
4. debate (verb/noun)   [de • bate]
    debat*able* (adjective)
5. encourage (verb)   [en • cour • age]
    encourage*ment* (noun)
6. estimate (verb/noun)   [es • ti • mate]
    estima*tion* (noun)
7. precious (adjective)   [pre • cious]
8. signify (verb)   [sig • ni • fy]
    signifi*cant* (adjective)
    signifi*cance* (noun)
    significant*ly* (adverb)

Summarizing a Science Passage
Content Words

summarize
    [summary]
main (points; ideas)
restate
identify
fluent
    [fluently]
skim
overall